INTERNATIONAL SOCIALISM ★

A quarterly journal of socialist theory

Summer 1992
Contents

**Issue 55 of INTERNATIONAL SOCIALISM, quarterly
journal of the Socialist Workers Party (Britain)**

Published June 1992
Copyright © International Socialism
Distribution/subscriptions: International Socialism,
PO Box 82, London E3.
American distribution/subscriptions: PO Box 16085, Chicago
Illinois 60616
Editorial and production: 071-538 1626/071-538 3307
Sales and subscriptions: 071-538 5821 x133
American sales: 312 666 7337

ISBN 0-906224-72-1

Printed by BPCC Wheatons Ltd, Exeter, England
Typeset by East End Offset, London E3

Cover design by Ian Goodyer

For details of back copies see the end pages of this book

Subscription rates for one year (four issues) are:

Britain and overseas (surface):	individual	£12.00 ($20)
	institutional	£20.00
Air speeded supplement:	North America	nil
	Europe/South America	£1.00
	elsewhere	£2.00

Note to contributors

The deadline for articles intended for issue 57 of
International Socialism is 1 September 1992

All contributions should be double-spaced with wide margins.
Please submit two copies. If you write your contribution
using a computer, please also supply a disk, together with
details of the computer and programme used.

INTERNATIONAL
SOCIALISM ★

A quarterly journal of socialist theory

THE RISE of fascism in Europe and the continuing centrality of racism to political life in every major capitalist country demands a clear and unambiguous response from the left. But what should that response be? What are the roots of racism? Is black nationalism or socialism the best way to defeat the racists?

Alex Callinicos addresses these issues and shows how questions of race are inextricably bound to questions of class. He examines the class position that lies behind black nationalism and develops a strategy that can unite black and white workers in a struggle for black liberation and socialism.

AMERICAN SOCIALIST Lee Sustar looks at some similar themes through an examination of the New York draft riots during the American Civil War. His review shows the forces pushing towards black and white unity and the strategies used by the establishment to tear that unity apart.

THE ELECTION in Britain has returned the Tories for a fourth term. Socialists need to take stock. Tony Cliff examines the balance of class forces, looks back on a decade where both the left and the right in the Labour Party failed to successfully challenge the Tories and concludes with a call to build a socialist alternative to Labour.

JOHN REES' 'In defence of October', published in *International Socialism* 52 has proven to be a controversial account of the Bolshevik revolution. Here we publish contributions from Robert Service, author of a biography of Lenin and *The Russian Revolution 1900-27*, Robin Blackburn, editor of *New Left Review*, Sam Farber, author of *Before Stalinism*, and David Finkel of the American magazine *Against the Current*, plus a rejoinder from John Rees.

Editor: John Rees, Assistant Editors: Alex Callinicos, Sue Clegg, Chris Harman, John Molyneux, Lindsey German, Pete Green, Costas Lapavitsas, Colin Sparks, Mike Gonzalez, Peter Morgan, Ruth Brown, Mike Haynes and Rob Hoveman.

Race and class

ALEX CALLINICOS

Racism remains one of the main features of the advanced capitalist societies. It is institutionalised in the systematic discrimination which black people experience in jobs, housing, the education system, and the harassment they suffer at the hands of police and immigration authorities. A striking development in European politics since the East European revolutions of 1989 has been the resurgence of racism, both in the unofficial form of the fascist and racist parties which have been able to make significant electoral gains recently (most notably in France, Germany and Belgium) and in the official form of the concerted attempts by European governments further to restrict immigration, most importantly by attacking the right to asylum. The more united European Community in which bourgeois politicians and even many socialists place their hopes will be Fortress Europe, its doors firmly closed to the impoverished masses of a Third World which most of the ex-Stalinist states seem in the process of joining. And the great Los Angeles rebellion at the end of April 1992 showed how race and class together have the potential to blow apart the structure of American society.

The stark fact that the rich capitalist democracies are profoundly racist societies demands action to challenge and, if possible, to abolish racism. Obviously, any anti-racist strategy presupposes an analysis of the nature and causes of racism. The traditional liberal view, still very influential, treats racism primarily as a matter of *attitudes*: the problem is that whites are prejudiced against black people. The obvious solution would seem then to be educating whites out of their prejudices; such a diagnosis is implicit in the programme of Racism Awareness Training (RAT) which, developed in the US in the 1970s, was taken up by a number of Labour councils in Britain during the 1980s.[1] At the same time the old liberal goal of integrating black minorities into their Western 'host' societies tended to be replaced by the idea of multiculturalism. This involved conceiving society as a collection of ethnic groups each with its own irreducibly different culture; the aim was now a pluralistic arrangement based on the mutual understanding by the different groups of each others' cultures, involving, in particular, an appreciation by the white majority of the value of non-European traditions.[2]

More radical anti-racists, by contrast, see racism not as a matter of the ideas in people's heads, but of *oppression*, of systematic inequalities in power and life chances stemming from an exploitative social structure; the solution lies therefore in political struggle, in the liberation of black people from their oppression. But within the radical camp there are vital differences in analysis and strategy. Black nationalists tend to see racism as an (at least relatively) autonomous phenomenon, whose origins, structure and dynamic, while connected to those of the capitalist mode of production, cannot be reduced to them; black liberation, the nationalists conclude, can be achieved only by black people themselves organised separately from white anti-racists. Revolutionary Marxists, by contrast, regard racism as a product of capitalism which serves to reproduce this social system by dividing the working class; it can be abolished, therefore, only through a socialist revolution achieved by a united working class, one in which blacks and whites join together against their common exploiter.[3]

Marxism: a Eurocentric tradition?

The difference between Marxism and black nationalism isn't always as starkly posed as this. Many black radicals have been influenced by versions of Marxism (usually some combination of Stalinism and academic Western Marxism). They draw on Marxist analyses of the slave trade and of imperialism, and argue that contemporary racism is of economic benefit to capitalism. Sometimes the kinship to Marxism seems very close. Thus A Sivanandan, editor of the journal *Race and Class* and one of the most influential black radical intellectuals in Britain, has written a splendid polemic against what he calls 'The Hokum of New Times', the capitulation to postmodernism that was virtually the last gasp of *Marxism Today*, now, happily, defunct.[4] But there are definite limits to this kinship. The conflict between Marxism and black nationalism is perhaps most systematically explored by Cedric Robinson, an American scholar associated with the Institute of Race Relations in London (of which Sivanandan is the director), in his book *Black Marxism*. Robinson's basic thesis is that Marxism is, in the very way in which its concepts are ordered, a Eurocentric ideology:

> *at base, that is to say at its epistemological substratum, Marxism is a Western construction—a conceptualisation of human affairs and historical development which is emergent from the historical experiences of European peoples mediated, in turn, through their civilisation, their social orders, and their cultures.*

Marxism, Robinson claims, isn't just European in its origins, but in 'its analytical presumptions, its historical perspectives, its points of view'. It consequently has failed to confront a 'recurring idea' in 'Western civilisation', namely racism and, in particular, the way in which 'racialism would inevitably permeate the social structures emergent from capitalism'. Twentieth century black radical intellectuals— Robinson traces the paths taken by three, WEB Du Bois, CLR James, and Richard Wright—have therefore had to work their way out of Marxism and rediscover an older tradition, 'the persistent and continuously evolving resistance of African peoples to oppression', for it is they, and not 'the European proletariat and its allies', which constitute the 'negation' of 'capitalist society'.[5]

It is easy enough to point out the flaws in Robinson's book, his constipated academic style, for example, and reliance on ex-Marxist poseurs like Jean Baudrillard and Cornelius Castoriadis and anti-Marxist liberals like Shlomo Avineri and Isaiah Berlin for the criticisms he advances of historical materialism. More seriously from the point of view of his own political project, Robinson's account of the black radical tradition verges on the mystical. 'The distinctions of political space and historical time have fallen away so that the making of one black collective identity suffuses nationalisms', he asserts. 'Harboured in the African Diaspora there is a single historical identity which is in opposition to the systemic privations of racial capitalism.' Robinson seems to be saying that all the struggles by black people against their oppression in both Africa and the New World have served to forge a shared identity, but when he comes to explain the nature of this identity Robinson descends ever deeper into obscurity, for example, declaring that the black radical tradition's 'focus was on the structures of the mind. Its epistemology granted supremacy to metaphysics not the material', whatever this means.[6] The real differences between forms of struggle—the attempts by maroons to survive at the margins of the slave colonies of the New World, the Haitian Revolution and other slave risings, the resistance by African polities to European colonial expansion, the great urban risings by American blacks in the 1960s, the contemporary struggle against apartheid, not to speak of the actual conflicts among black people—say, between a supporter of the ANC and Inkatha in Johannesburg or Durban—are all dissolved into a single vague abstract 'identity'.

The challenge posed by Robinson and his co-thinkers nevertheless remains. Can the classical Marxist tradition of Marx and Engels, Lenin and Trotsky, provide an analysis of racism capable of providing the basis of an effective strategy for black liberation? This article is an attempt to meet that challenge.

The modernity of racism

Racism is a historical novelty, characteristic of modern capitalist societies. This claim is central to the Marxist analysis of racism; it is, correspondingly, denied by many black nationalists. Robinson, for example, claims that racism is not a capitalist but a peculiarly European phenomenon: 'Racialism insinuated not only mediaeval, feudal and capitalist social structures, forms of property, and modes of production, but as well the very values and traditions of consciousness through which the peoples of these ages came to understand their worlds and their experiences.'[7] Similarly, the black American scholar Manning Marable argues that 'racism and patriarchy are both *precapitalist* in their social and ideological origin.'[8] The implication is that racism would survive the overthrow of capitalism, and that consequently an autonomous black movement is necessary to eradicate it.

To appreciate why this view is mistaken we must first consider the nature of racism. Racism exists where a group of people is discriminated against on the basis of characteristics which are held to be inherent in them as a group. Racism is often associated with a difference in the skin colour of the oppressors and the oppressed, but this is by no means a necessary condition of racism. Irish people were the victims of racism in 19th century Britain despite being as white as the 'natives'. Modern anti-semitism is another case of racism which is not based on colour differences. There is a sense in which difference in skin colour isn't even a sufficient condition for the existence of racism. Where it is involved it is as part of a complex of characteristics—for example, inferior intelligence, laziness, overactive sexuality, in the case of the traditional Western stereotype of Africans—which are imputed to the oppressed group and which serve to justify their oppression. It is the idea of some systematic set of differences between oppressor and oppressed, of which any visible physical differences are part, that is important rather than the physical differences themselves.

What confuses the matter is that classical racist ideology tends to highlight supposed physical differences between groups of people. The most theoretically articulated version of racist ideology is what Peter Fryer calls the 'pseudo-scientific mythology of race' that flourished in Britain (and indeed the rest of the developed capitalist world) between the 1840s and the 1940s. This held that humankind was divided into races each based on distinct biological characteristics and that the domination of the world by Western imperialism reflected the inherent superiority of the white races over the rest in the process of natural selection.[9]

Now the idea of biologically distinct races has no scientific basis:

> *Of all human genetic variation known for enzymes and other proteins, where it has been possible to actually count up the frequencies of different forms of the genes and so get an objective estimate of genetic variation, 85 percent turns out to be between individuals within the same local population, tribe, or nation; a further 8 percent is between tribes or nations within a major 'race'; and the remaining 7 percent is between major 'races'. This means that the genetic variation between one Spaniard and another, or between one Masai and another, is 85 percent of all human genetic variation, while only 15 percent is accounted for by breaking up people into groups... Any use of racial categories must take its justifications from some other source than biology. The remarkable feature of human evolution and history has been the very small degree of divergence between geographical populations as compared with genetic variation among individuals.[10]*

Racial differences are *invented*: that is, they emerge as part of a historically specific relationship of oppression in order to justify the existence of that relationship. So what is the historical peculiarity of racism as a form of oppression? In the first instance, it is that the characteristics which justify discrimination are held to be *inherent* in the oppressed group. A victim of racism can't change herself and thus avoid oppression; black people, for example, can't change their colour. This represents an important difference between, for example, racial and religious oppression, since one solution for someone persecuted on religious grounds is to change their faith.

Judith Herrin observes:

> *As the ancient world collapsed, faith rather than imperial rule became the feature that identified the universe, what Christians called the*

oikoumene, and Muslims, **Dar al Islam**. Religion had fused the political, social, and cultural into self-contained systems, separated by their differences of faith.[11]

The Mediterranean world (and its extensions in northern and central Europe and in central Asia) thus became polarised between two rival civilisations, Islam and Christendom, whose conflict spanned ten centuries, from the Arab conquest of much of the eastern Roman Empire soon after Muhammed's death in 632 until the second siege of Vienna in 1683. But despite the ferocity of this struggle it was not a racial struggle. Conversions from one faith to the other sometimes occurred. During the Crusades Christian and Muslim rulers often struck alliances, and at the height of the Ottoman threat to Christendom in the 16th century the King of France tended to support the Turkish Sultan in his struggle with the Habsburg rulers of Spain as a way of weakening a dangerous European rival.

Adherents to faiths other than the dominant one were often discriminated against or persecuted in various ways: the most notable instances in the case of mediaeval Christendom were perhaps the widespread massacres of Jews at the time of the First Crusade at the end of the 11th century and the extermination of the Cathars of Languedoc at the beginning of the 13th century. Nevertheless religious persecution of this kind was not the same as racial oppression. This is perhaps best brought out by the case of the Jews. What Hannah Arendt calls 'the assumption of an eternal anti-semitism', according to which 'outbursts need no special explanation because they are natural consequences of an eternal problem', is quite widespread.[12] On this view, the Holocaust takes its place as merely the latest case of 2,000 years of anti-semitism. But, as Zygmunt Bauman points out, while in pre-modern Europe Jews were in a peculiarly vulnerable position because of their status as religious outsiders, this 'did not on the whole prevent their accommodation into the prevailing social order... In a society divided into estates or castes the Jews were just one estate or caste among many. The individual Jew was defined by the caste to which he belonged, and by the specific privileges or burdens the caste enjoyed or bore. But the same applied to every other member of the same society.'[13] Modern anti-semitism developed in the 19th century against the background of the collapse of this hierarchical order of estates, and treated the Jew no longer as a religious outsider but as a member of a biologically inferior *race*. It was the emergence of racial anti-semitism which made the Nazi 'Final Solution' conceivable in ideological terms. In Arendt's words, 'Jews had been able to escape from Judaism [religion] into conversion; from Jewishness [race] there was no escape.'[14]

There is thus no escape from racial oppression for members of the subordinate 'race'. Now this form of oppression is peculiar to capitalist societies.[15] It must be distinguished from a pervasive feature of pre-capitalist societies, namely prejudices against strangers. Most people before the advent of industrial capitalism were peasants living in small rural communities. Poor communications meant that contact with anywhere outside an extremely narrow radius was rare. The result was often an intense, even suffocating, involvement in each others' lives within the peasant community, combined with deep ignorance and suspicion of strangers. What Bauman calls 'heterophobia' (resentment of the different), is not the same as modern racism: 'In a world that boasts the unprecedented ability to improve human conditions by reorganising human affairs on a rational basis, racism manifests the conviction that a certain category of human beings cannot be incorporated into the rational order, whatever the effort.'[16]

What is striking about the slave and feudal societies of precapitalist Europe is, contrary to the claims of Robinson and Marable, the absence of ideologies and practices which excluded and subordinated a particular group on the grounds of their inherent inferiority. We have already seen that mediaeval Europe conceived of itself as Christendom, from which Jews, Muslims and pagans were excluded by their religious beliefs, not their race. Similarly, the slave societies of classical antiquity do not seem to have relied on racism to justify the wholesale use of chattel slaves to provide the ruling class with its surplus product. The black American historian Frank M Snowden Jnr writes: 'Social intercourse [between black and white] did not give rise among the Greeks and Romans to the colour prejudices of certain later Western societies. The Greeks and Romans developed no theories of white superiority.'[17] The most striking instance of the absence of racism based on colour in classical antiquity is provided by the case of Septimius Severus, Roman Emperor from AD 193 to 211, who was almost certainly black. One of the main characteristics of Roman rule was the effort to incorporate local aristocracies into an imperial ruling class sharing a culture which fused the Greek and Roman traditions.

Another case in point is provided by Martin Bernal's book *Black Athena*, which has had an enormous impact on black radicals. Bernal seeks to rehabilitate what he calls the 'Ancient Model', according to which 'Greek culture had arisen as a result of colonisation, around 1500 BC, by Egyptians and Phoenicians who had civilised the inhabitants.' He argues that this was the generally accepted interpretation of the origins of classical Greece until the late 18th century, when it was supplanted by the 'Aryan Model', which asserted that 'there had been an invasion from the north—unreported in ancient tradition—which had overwhelmed the local "Aegean" or "pre-Hellenic" culture. Greek civilisation is seen as the result of the mixture of the Indo-European speaking Hellenes and their indigenous subjects.' Bernal claims that the overthrow of the Ancient Model was a consequence of the rise of racism, whose theorists sought to trace the origins of the modern European nations to barbarian invasions by Aryan peoples from the north, similar to the influx of German tribes which contributed to the fall of the Roman Empire in the west:

> For 18th and 19th century Romantics and racists it was simply intolerable for Greece, which was seen not merely as the epitome of Europe but also as its pure childhood, to have been the result of the mixture of native Europeans and colonising Africans and Semites. Therefore the Ancient Model had to be overthrown and replaced by something more acceptable.[18]

The political significance of *Black Athena* is obvious enough. It would be a powerful blow against Western racism if it could indeed be shown that classical Greece, which still occupies a sanctified position as the origin of European civilisation, was an offshoot of more advanced societies in Africa and Asia. There is indeed much evidence especially of Asian influence during the archaic period (800-500 BC), which preceded the full flowering of classical Greece after the defeat of the Persian invasions at the beginning of the 5th century BC.[19] The weakness of Bernal's argument is that he concentrates on tracing Egyptian and Phoenician influences on *individual* practices or institutions—the role of African and Asian colonisers in founding particular religious cults or cities, the trace elements of Egyptian and Phoenician in the Greek language itself. What this misses out is the distinctive nature of classical Greek society as a *totality*, characterised by reliance on slave labour as the main source of ruling class income and the political institution of the city state based on citizen armies of heavy infantry.[20] Whatever the economic contacts, cultural influences and direct colonisations from outside which contributed to the emergence of classical Greece, it represented a different form of society from those which preceded and surrounded it in the Eastern Mediterranean.

However this may be, there is one very striking aspect of Bernal's case. This is the fact that, as he constantly reiterates, 'the "Ancient Model" was the conventional view among Greeks in the Classical and Hellenistic ages.'[21] Its most important source is Herodotus's *Histories*, which sought to explain the Persian Wars, which provided classical Greece with its own epic, comparable to those of Homer, by exploring the Greeks' relations with Asia and Africa. Despite the fact that the climax of his book is devoted to the struggle between the Greek city states and the Persian Empire, Herodotus constantly stresses the Greeks' dependence on African and Asian influences. For example, he argues that Greek religion had its origins in Egypt: his respect for this far more ancient civilisation is evident.[22] A similar attitude informs Herodotus's treatment of Persia itself. As Arnoldo Momigliano puts it, 'Herodotus respects the Persians and considers them capable of thinking like Greeks...his thinking is basically committed to the mutual understanding of Greeks and Persians.'[23] Whether or not the Ancient Model offers, as Bernal claims, an accurate account of the origins of classical Greece, the belief, expressed most systematically by Herodotus, in the Greeks' historical debt to their African and Asian neighbours is an indication of the absence of any ideology of racial exclusivity and superiority in antiquity.

Slavery and the development of capitalism

Racism as we know it today developed during a key phase in the development of capitalism as the dominant mode of production on a global scale—the establishment during the 17th and 18th centuries of colonial plantations in the New World using slave labour imported from Africa to produce consumer goods such as tobacco and sugar and industrial inputs such as cotton for the world market. Peter Fryer has traced its development in Britain: 'Racism emerged in the oral tradition in Barbados in the 17th century and crystallised in print in Britain in the 18th, as the ideology of the plantocracy, the class of sugar-planters and slave-merchants that dominated England's Caribbean colonies.'[24] The most influential statement of this ideology was provided by Edward Long in his *History of Jamaica* (1774), but already in 1753 the great Scottish philosopher David Hume, one of the giants of the 18th century Enlightenment, had declared: 'I am apt to suspect the negroes, and in general all the other species of men (for there are four or five different kinds) to be naturally inferior to the whites.'[25]

The development of what Robin Blackburn calls 'systemic slavery' in the plantations of North America and the West Indies, requiring the import of some 6 million African captives in the 18th century alone, is one of capitalism's greatest crimes.[26] It is, however, a common argument that it was the prior existence of racism which led to the exploitation of *African* slaves. This interpretation was challenged by Eric Williams in his classic study of the subject: 'Slavery was not born of racism: rather, racism was the consequence of slavery. Unfree labour in the New World was brown, white, black, and yellow; Catholic, Protestant and pagan.'[27] Indeed, the plantation economies initially relied on unfree *white* labour in the shape of indentured servants, who agreed to work for a particular master on a servile basis for three to five years, in exchange for free passage from Europe. According to Blackburn:

more than half the white emigrants to colonial North America arrived as indentured servants; the French and British Caribbean also absorbed tens of thousands of these tied labourers, who could be purchased more cheaply than slaves. Altogether some 350,000 servants were shipped to the British colonies up to the 1770s.[28]

Barbara Fields argues that the tobacco plantations of colonial Virginia 'rested primarily on the backs of English indentured servants, not African slaves', until the late 17th century:

Indentured servants served longer terms in Virginia than their English counterparts and enjoyed less dignity and less protection in law and custom. They could be bought and sold like livestock, kidnapped, stolen, put up as stakes in card games, and awarded—even before their arrival in America—to the victors in lawsuits. Greedy magnates (if the term is not redundant) stinted the servants' food and cheated them out of their freedom dues, and often out of their freedom itself, when they had served their time. Servants were beaten, maimed, and even killed with impunity.[29]

As Fields observes, 'the only degradation' white servants 'were spared was perpetual enslavement along with their issue in perpetuity'. This was their chief disadvantage to plantation owners concerned to secure a stable, long term labour supply to meet the growing demand for colonial products. But, Fields argues, it was not their colour which prevented the indentured servants' full scale enslavement, but the limits on landowners' power imposed by 'centuries of day-to-day contest, overt and covert, armed and unarmed, peaceable and forcible' between exploiters and exploited in England:

To have degraded the servants into slaves en masse would have driven the continuing struggle up several notches, a dangerous undertaking considering that the servants were well-armed, that they outnumbered their masters, and that the Indians could easily take advantage of the inevitably resulting warfare among the enemy. Moreover, the enslavement of already arrived immigrants, once news of it reached England, would have threatened the sources of future immigration. Even the greediest and most short-sighted profiteer could foresee disaster in any such policy.[30]

The solution to the planters' problems of labour supply was provided from the 1680s onwards by 'the importation of African labourers in larger and larger numbers', which 'made it possible to maintain a sufficient corps of plantation labourers without building up an explosive charge of armed Englishmen resentful at being denied the rights of Englishmen and disposing of the material and political resources to make their resentment felt.'[31] Racism developed in the context created by the development of the 'systemic slavery' of the New World: the idea that Africans were (in Hume's words) 'naturally inferior' to whites justified denying them 'the rights of Englishmen' and enslaving them. But this raises another question. Why was it necessary to justify slavery in the first place? This may seem like an odd question, until we consider the other main historical example of a society based on slave labour, classical antiquity. Ellen Wood observes:

> Some people may be surprised to learn that in ancient Greece and Rome, despite the almost universal acceptance of slavery, the idea that slavery was justified by natural inequalities among human beings never caught on. The one notable exception, Aristotle's conception of natural slavery, never gained currency. The more common view seems to have been that slavery is a convention, though a useful one, which was justifiable simply on the grounds of its usefulness. In fact, it was even conceded that this useful institution was **contrary to nature**. Such a view appears not only in Greek philosophy but was even recognised in Roman law. It has even been suggested that slavery was the only case in Roman law where there was a n acknowledged conflict between the **ius gentium**, the conventional law of nations, and the **ius naturale**, the law of nature.[32]

Why did the ideologues of Greece and Rome find it unnecessary to come up with any elaborate justification of what they acknowledged to be an 'unnatural' institution? To answer this question we must keep in mind one of the basic features of precapitalist class societies, namely their reliance on what Marx called 'extra-economic force'. Whatever their differences, the slave and feudal modes of production, for example, both rest on the exploitation of unfree labour: the slave is reduced to the status of a chattel, while the feudal peasant is subject to his lord's military and judicial power, which is used to extract his surplus labour in the form of rent.[33] The nature of exploitation in these societies was reflected in their hierarchical organisation and the division of the population into legally unequal groups—citizen and slave in classical antiquity (and indeed the citizens themselves were divided, for example, between the *honestiores* and *humiliores* under the Roman Empire), the estates of mediaeval Europe. Inequality of a visible, systematic, legally entrenched kind was the *norm* in precapitalist societies. Their ideologues took it for granted, and tended to depict society as based on a division of labour in which even the most humble had their allocated role. Plato's *Republic*, with its hierarchy of Guardians, Warriors and Labourers, is the classic Western version of this ideology. Another example is quoted by the great mediaeval Arab philosopher, Ibn Khaldûn:

The world is a garden the fence of which is the dynasty. The dynasty is an authority through which life is given to proper behaviour. Proper behaviour is a policy directed by the ruler. The ruler is an institution supported by the soldiers. The soldiers are helpers, who are maintained by money. Money is sustenance brought together by the subjects. The subjects are servants protected by justice. Justice is something familiar, and, through it, the world persists. The world is a garden...[34]

In such hierarchical societies slavery was merely one of a spectrum of unequal statuses, requiring no special explanation. Not so in capitalist society. For the capitalist mode of production rests on the exploitation of *free* wage labour. The wage labourer is, Marx says, 'free in a double sense, free from the old relations of clientship, bondage and servitude, and secondly free of all belongings and possessions, and of every objective, material form, *free of all property*'.[35] It is not the workers' legal and political subordination to the exploiter, but their separation from the means of production, and the resulting economic compulsion to sell their only productive resource, labour power, that is the basis of capitalist exploitation. The worker and capitalist confront each other in the labour market as legal equals. Workers are perfectly free not to sell their labour power: it is only the fact that the alternative is starvation or the dole which leads them to do so. Hence the labour market is, as Marx puts it, 'a very Eden of the innate rights of man', 'the exclusive realm of Freedom, Equality, Property, and Bentham'. It is only in 'the hidden abode of production' that exploitation takes place.[36]

This contrast between the formal equality and the real inequality of capitalist and worker is a fundamental feature of bourgeois society, reflected in many aspects of its development. The great bourgeois revolutions, which swept away the obstacles to the dominance of the capitalist mode of production, mobilised the masses under the banner of freedom and equality. 'The poorest he that is in England has a life to live as the greatest he, and therefore...every man that is to live under a government ought first by his own consent to put himself under that government,' said Colonel Rainsborough in the Putney Debates of 1647. 'We hold these truths to be self-evident, that all men are created equal, that they are endowed by their Creator with certain unalienable rights, that among these are life, liberty, and the pursuit of happiness', the American Declaration of Independence of 1776 proclaims. And the Great French Revolution of 1789 was waged under the banner of *Liberté, Égalité, Fraternité.*

And yet the paradox was that capitalism, whose domination involves the exploitation of free wage labour, benefited enormously during a critical phase in its development from colonial slavery. This relationship continued well into the era of the Industrial Revolution, the textile factories of whose heartland in northern England imported their main raw material from the slave plantations of the American South. Capitalism's reliance on slave labour became an anomaly requiring explanation. It was in this context that the idea that blacks were sub-human and therefore did not demand the equal respect increasingly acknowledged as the right of human beings, began to take hold.

Barbara Fields argues that 'racial ideology' took hold especially among the 'white yeomanry' in the southern US—the small farmers and artisans who, representing nearly two thirds of the population of the Old South, largely did not own slaves and sought to assert their claim to political and economic independence of the planters:

> Racial ideology supplied the means of explaining slavery to people whose terrain was a republic founded on radical doctrines of liberty and natural rights; and, more important, a republic in which those doctrines seemed to represent accurately the world in which all but a minority lived. Only when the denial of liberty became an anomaly apparent even to the least obser-vant and reflective members of Euro-American society did ideology system-atically explain the anomaly.[37]

Similarly, Peter Fryer shows how racism emerged in 18th century Britain 'as a largely defensive ideology—the weapon of a class whose wealth, way of life, and power were under mounting attack'.[38] Racist ideologues such as Long wrote to defend the West Indian planters from the growing pressures to abolish, not just the slave trade, but the very institution of slavery itself. Yet racist ideology survived abolition, and indeed received further theoretical elaboration in the shape of the pseudo-scientific biology of races which drew on a vulgarised version of Darwin's theory of natural selection. This reflected that the anomaly which had given rise to racism in the first place continued to exist in another form, the domination of the world by a handful of European (or, in the case of the US and Russia, Europeanised) powers. This state of affairs was justified by the idea that the biological constitution of Asians and Africans suited them to rule by the white 'races', whose duty it was to govern the world in the interests of their subjects. The classic statement of this view is, of course, Kipling's poem 'The White Man's Burden', written in 1898 as an appeal to the US, then just begin-ning its career as an imperial power, to:

> Take up the White Man's burden—
> Send forth the best ye breed—
> Go bind your sons to exile
> To serve your captives' need;

To wait in heavy harness
On fluttered folk and wild—
Your new-caught, sullen peoples,
Half devil and half child.[39]

Racism in contemporary capitalism

Racism is thus a creature of slavery and empire, which developed in order to justify the denial to the colonial oppressed of the equal rights that capitalism tended to promise all of humankind. The argument so far therefore establishes a historical connection between racism and capitalism. But what about racism today? Simply to halt the analysis at this point would leave contemporary racism as some sort of hangover from the past which had somehow managed to survive the abolition of slavery and the collapse of the colonial empires. This, at any rate, seems to be Peter Fryer's view: 'Long after the material conditions that originally gave rise to racist ideology had ceased to exist, these dead ideas went on gripping the minds of the living. They led to various kinds of racist behaviour on the part of many white people in Britain, including white people in authority.'[40] This analysis, asserting as it does that racism no longer has any material foundations, implies that the main task of anti-racists, among white people at any rate, is to change attitudes, presumably through some process of education. It is mistaken, however: the material conditions of modern capitalism continue to give rise to racism.

Let's note, in the first place, a change in racist ideology. Martin Barker is one of a number of writers to have noted the emergence of what he calls the 'new racism', which highlights, not the biological superiority of some races to others, but the cultural differences among 'ethnic' groups.[41] The ideologues of the Tory right, from Enoch Powell to Norman Tebbit, have used the idea that the cultural differences between European and non-European peoples make it impossible for them to live together in the same society to justify tighter immigration controls and even (in Powell's case) the repatriation of black people. But the most notorious example of this variant of racism is, of course, Mrs Thatcher's remark during an interview on *World in Action* on 30 January 1978: 'People are really afraid that this country might be rather swamped by people with a different culture.'

How big a change does the 'new racism' represent, and what caused its emergence? To start with the latter question, as we have seen, the idea that humankind is divided into races with different biological constitutions is no longer scientifically respectable. It is, moreover, positively disreputable morally and politically because of the use the Nazis made of it. The Holocaust made biological racism in its 19th century form stink—hence the shift from biology to culture, and from race to ethnicity. The change must not, however, be overstated. In the first place, biological racism is still around, for example, in sociobiology's attempts to explain social inequalities in biological terms and in the idea that American blacks' poor scores in IQ tests reflect genetic differences between them and whites.[42] Secondly, the idea that blacks are naturally inferior to whites is still very much part of popular racism, though it tends to use the idea of cultural differences as a respectable cloak. Often certain apparently innocent words used in public pronouncements represent a tacit coded appeal to cruder racist attitudes. Thatcher's use of the word 'swamp' is a case in point: it's surely no accident that the police operation, involving large scale harassment of blacks, which sparked the Brixton riot of April 1981 was called 'Swamp 81'.

Thirdly, the 'cultural' or 'ethnic identities' which have taken the place of 'race' in polite discussion tend to involve the same kind of crude stereotypes characteristic of old fashioned racism.[43] 'Ethnicity' or 'culture' is conceived as a fate from which those it embraces cannot escape. Although acknowledged as a product of (usually caricatured) history, it is no longer amenable to further change by human action: it has become effectively part of nature. At most those in one 'ethnic' prison can try to understand other people's prisons (multiculturalism), or they can exchange prisons, as Tebbit demanded of black people when he proposed his 'cricket test', which amounted to insisting that, if they want to be regarded as British, they must, in effect, break all connections with the countries from which they or their ancestors emigrated and assimilate to the dominant culture—a test which he assumed most would fail.[44]

Modern racism, with its rhetoric of cultural difference and usually tacit appeal to older notions of natural inferiority, in any case arises in the conditions of industrial capitalism. Capitalism in its fully developed form rests on the exploitation of free wage labour. But the working class which sells its labour power to capital is internally composite in two ways. First of all, the technical division of labour requires a workforce with different kinds of skill; one of the functions of the labour market is to meet this requirement, variations in wage rates serving as a means of allocating different kinds of labour power. Secondly, to secure an adequate supply of labour capitalists are often forced to reach beyond the borders of the state in question, drawing towards them workers of different national origin. Eric Hobsbawm has pointed out that 'the middle of the 19th century marks the beginning of the greatest migration of peoples in history', starting with the great flood of European immigrants to the US, and to a lesser extent South America, Australasia and South Africa.[45] The most spectacular result is the US itself, the proverbial 'nation of immigrants', its working class entirely formed from successive waves of immigration. But there are many other cases, ranging from the role of Irish migrant labour in Victorian Britain to the large scale use of Polish labourers by Prussian landowners in the late 19th century. Reliance on immigrant labour has proved to be a structural feature of advanced capitalism in the second half of the 20th century. By the early 1970s there were nearly 11 million immigrants in Western Europe, who had come from southern Europe or former colonies during the boom of the 1950s and 1960s.[46] And even during the crisis ridden 1970s and 1980s the US economy continued to suck in a vast new immigration from Latin America and east Asia.

Capitalists employ immigrant workers because of the economic benefits they bring: they contribute to the flexibility of labour supply, are often unable to refuse employment in low paid, dirty and dangerous jobs frequently involving shiftwork, and, since the costs of their upbringing have been met in their country of origin, make, through the taxes they pay, a net contribution to the reproduction of labour power in the 'host' country.[47] But, more than that, the existence of a working class composed of 'natives' and immigrants (or, in the case of countries like the US, largely of less and more recent immigrants) makes possible the division of that class on racial lines, particularly if differences in national origin at least partially correspond to different positions in the technical division of labour (for example, between craft workers and unskilled labourers).

Marx grasped the way in which racial divisions between 'native' and immigrant workers could weaken the working class, as he showed in his famous letter of 9 April 1870 to Meyer and Vogt. Here Marx seeks to explain why the Irish struggle for self determination was a vital issue for the British working class:

*And most important of all! Every industrial and commercial centre in England possesses a working class **divided** into two hostile camps, English proletarians and Irish proletarians. The ordinary English worker hates the Irish worker as a competitor who lowers his standard of life. In relation to the Irish worker he feels himself a member of the **ruling** nation and so turns himself into a tool of the aristocrats and capitalists of his country **against Ireland**, thus strengthening their domination **over himself**. He cherishes religious, social, and national prejudices against the Irish worker. His attitude towards him is much the same as that of the 'poor whites' to the 'niggers' in the former slave states of the USA. The Irishman pays him back with interest in his own money. He sees in the English worker at once the accomplice and stupid tool of the **English rule in Ireland**.*

This antagonism is artificially kept alive and intensified by the press, the pulpit, the comic papers, in short by all the means at the disposal of the *ruling classes. This **antagonism** is the **secret of the impotence of the English working class**, despite its organisation. It is the secret by which the capitalist class maintains its power. And that class is fully aware of it.*[48]

In this remarkable passage Marx sketches out the outline of a materialist explanation of racism in modern capitalism. We can take him as identifying three main conditions of existence of racism:

i) *Economic competition between workers* ('the ordinary English worker hates the Irish worker as a competitor who lowers his standard of life'). A particular pattern of capital accumulation implies a specific distribution of labour which is reflected in the labour market by different wage rates. Particularly in periods of capital restructuring when labour is deskilled, capitalists (being what they are) are tempted to replace established skilled workers with cheaper and less skilled workers. If the two groups of workers have different national origins, and probably therefore also different languages and traditions, the potential exists for the development of racial antagonisms among the two groups of workers. This is a pattern which has repeated itself often enough in the history of the American working class.[49] The racial divisions involved need not, however, arise from the attempt by skilled workers to defend their position. On a number of occasions in the 19th and early 20th centuries American blacks were driven out of the skilled niches they had managed to attain by white workers—for example, by unskilled Irish immigrants in the period before the civil war.[50]

ii) *The appeal of racist ideology to white workers* ('the ordinary English worker...feels himself a member of the *ruling* nation'). The mere fact of economic competition between different groups of workers is not enough to explain the development of racial antagonisms. Why do racist ideas appeal to white workers? One answer is that it reflects their economic interest in racial oppression: white workers, in other words, benefit materially from racism. This explanation is, I argue below, mistaken. The basis of another, better, explanation is sketched out by WEB Du Bois in his great work *Black Reconstruction in America* (1935). Du Bois was trying to account for the division among black and white workers after the defeat of Radical Reconstruction—the efforts by an alliance of ex-slaves and white radicals to uproot racism in the American South after the civil war. He argues that:

the [Marxist] theory of labouring class unity...failed to work in the South...because the theory of race was supplemented by a carefully planned and slowly evolved method, which drove such a wedge between the white and black workers that there probably are not today in the world two groups of workers with practically identical interests who hate and fear each other so deeply and persistently and who are kept so far apart that neither sees anything of common interest.

It must be remembered that the white group of labourers, while they received a low wage, were compensated for by a sort of public and psychological wage. They were given public deference and titles of courtesy because they were white. They were admitted freely with all classes of white people to public functions, public parks, and public schools. The police were drawn from their ranks, and the courts, dependent upon their votes, treated them with leniency as to encourage lawlessness. Their vote selected public officials, and while this had small effect upon the economic situation, it had great effect upon their personal treatment and the deference shown them. White schoolhouses were the best in the community, and conspicuously placed, and they cost anywhere from twice to ten times as much per capita as the coloured schools. The newspapers specialised in news that flattered the poor whites and almost utterly ignored the Negro except in crime and ridicule.

On the other hand, in the same way, the Negro was subject to public insult; was afraid of mobs; was liable to the jibes of children and the unreasoning fears of white women; and compelled almost continuously to submit to various badges of inferiority. The result of this was that the wages of both classes could be kept low, the whites fearing to be supplanted by Negro labour, the Negroes always being threatened by the substitution of white labour.[51]

Du Bois is concerned here with a peculiarly extreme case of racism—the American South in the era of Jim Crow, so powerfully depicted by Richard Wright in books like *Uncle Tom's Children*. But his argument permits a more general extension. It has two elements. First, racism meant that 'two groups of workers with practically identical interests' were divided, so that 'the wages of both classes could be kept low'; Du Bois thus argues that, contrary to the black nationalists like Cedric Robinson who want to claim him for their own, white workers don't have an interest in the oppression of blacks (a view emphatically shared by another contributor to Robinson's supposed 'black radical tradition', CLR James).[52] Secondly, white workers received, in compensation for their low wages, 'a sort of public and psychological wage' deriving from their membership of what Marx calls 'the *ruling* nation'.

Marx in fact provides the means to understand the mechanism involved in this process of compensation in a famous passage in the 1843 Introduction to his *Contribution to the Critique of Hegel's Philosophy of Right*:'Religious distress is at the same time the *expression* of real distress and also the *protest* against real distress. Religion is the sigh of the oppressed creature, the heart of a heartless world, just as it is the spirit of spiritless conditions. It is the *opium* of the people.'[53] Religious beliefs are thus not just an invention foisted on the masses by a clerical conspiracy, as the philosophers of the Enlightenment had argued; they are accepted because they provide an imaginary solution of real contradictions. Religion offers solace for the ills of this world in a heavenly world beyond the grave. Its power lies in its recognition of the existence of suffering and oppression, even though its solution is a false one. Marx here uncovers one of the mechanisms at work in ideologies in general, including racist ideology. Racism offers white workers the comfort of believing themselves part of the dominant group; it also provides, in times of crisis, a ready made scapegoat, in the shape of the oppressed group.

Racism thus gives white workers a particular identity, and one moreover which unites them with white capitalists. We have here, then, a case of the kind of 'imagined community' discussed by Benedict Anderson in his influential analysis of nationalism. The nation, he argues, is 'an imagined political community': in particular, 'regardless of the actual inequality and exploitation that may prevail in each, the nation is always conceived as a deep horizontal comradeship'. Anderson, however, stresses what he sees as the differences between nationalism and racism. 'The fact of the matter', he writes, 'is that nationalism thinks in terms of historical destinies, while racism dreams of eternal contaminations, transmitted from the origins of time through an endless sequence of loathsome copulations: outside history.'[54] It is undoubtedly true that, as we have seen, racist ideology conceives race (or, more recently, ethnicity) as inescapable fate. Nevertheless, Anderson's argument fails to take into account the way in which in recent decades the idea of the *national* culture has become one of the main reasons used to justify, for example, tightening up immigration controls: consider Thatcher's infamous appeal to those afraid of being 'swamped by people with a different culture', discussed above.[55]

From a broader historical perspective, moreover, the crucial phase in the development of popular nationalism in the advanced capitalist countries came in the late 19th century, as part of the process through which the European ruling classes sought to incorporate newly enfranchised, increasingly organised workers within the same community.[56] Against a background of growing competition among the imperialist powers, workers were encouraged to identify their interests with those of 'their' ruling classes in these rivalries. It was in this same period that the pseudo-scientific biology of race received its most developed formulation: it served not merely to justify Western imperialist domination of the world, but also to sanctify the conflicts among the great powers as one aspect of the struggle for survival among the races.

Racism buttressed nationalism, leading workers to see themselves as members, like their exploiters, of the higher races which were fighting each other for supremacy of the world. Anderson is right to insist that nationalism in general is not the same as racism—many nationalists, particularly those involved in struggles for colonial liberation, have combined an identification with their own nations with a sincere belief in the equality of peoples, but imperialist nationalism provides a breeding ground where, in the right conditions, racism can grow.

iii) *The efforts of the capitalist class to establish and maintain racial divisions among workers* ('this antagonism is kept artificially alive by the press, the pulpit, the comic papers, in short by all the means at the disposal of the ruling classes'). Marx makes it clear that racism is in the interests of capital, calling it 'the secret by which the capitalist class maintains its power' and stressing that 'that class is fully aware of it'. This sounds a bit as if Marx is saying that racism is just the result of a capitalist conspiracy. This is not so. As we have seen, there is an objective economic context of racial divisions, namely capital's constantly changing demands for different kinds of labour which can often only be met through immigration. We have also seen that racism offers for workers of the oppressed 'race' the imaginary compensation for the exploitation they suffer of belonging to the *'ruling* nation'. It is, moreover, an objective fact about capitalism that racism helps keep capitalism going by dividing and therefore weakening the working class. The adage, 'Divide and rule', is an ancient piece of ruling class wisdom, coined by the Roman Emperor Tiberius in the 1st century AD. Capitalist domination does not occur automatically—it must actively be organised. One way of doing this is through promoting racism. It happens all the time: think of George Bush's cynical use of racism (the TV ads about Willie Horton) to help win the 1988 presidential campaign in the US. Capitalism isn't just a bosses' conspiracy, but capitalists do quite often resort to racism to divide the working class.[57]

Black and white workers

Racism, then, helps to keep capitalism going. It is thus in the interests of the capitalist class. But what about the working class? Perhaps the single most important difference between Marxists and black nationalists is that the latter believe that white workers materially benefit from racism. The other side of this belief tends to be the idea of a black movement which transcends class divisions. This is theorised in various ways. Cedric Robinson argues that the agency of revolutionary change is not the industrial working class but the 'black radical tradition' articulating the 'black collective identity' forged by centuries of resistance.

'The experimentation with Western political inventories of change, specifically nationalism and class struggle, is coming to a close. Black radicalism is transcending those traditions in order to adhere to its own authority.'[58] Paul Gilroy takes Marxists to task for positing 'a complete discontinuity...between the interests of the black *petit bourgeois* and working-class black settlers on the basis of their objectively contradictory class position'. 'Dogmatism' of this kind ignores 'the construction of the Black Community as a complex and inclusive collectivity with a distinctive political language'.[59] Sivanandan is committed to a much more robust form of class analysis, yet his primary focus is on 'the new underclass of homeworkers and sweatshop workers, casual and part-time workers, *ad hoc* and temporary workers, thrown up by the putting-out system in retailing, the flexi-system in manufacturing, and the hire and fire system in the expanding service sector' rather than the entire working class, white as well as black.[60]

Denying that white workers have an interest in fighting racism is often justified by resorting to the idea that they form a privileged labour aristocracy benefiting from imperialist super-profits extracted from Third World toilers. As originally formulated independently by Lenin and Du Bois during the First World War, the theory of the labour aristocracy was an attempt to explain reformism by arguing that it reflected the material interests of a *layer* of the Western working class.[61] In the hands of the black nationalists, however, it becomes the idea that *all* workers in the advanced economies share in the fruits of imperialism. Thus Ron Ramdin declares that 'the exploitation and degradation of the colonial working class was an indispensable requirement in maintaining the standard of living of the British working class.'[62]

The idea is, however, completely untenable. In the first place, the theory of the labour aristocracy is an extremely poor guide to the behaviour of the Western working class during the heyday of classical imperialism in the late 19th and early 20th centuries. Aside from the flaws in its economic arguments, the theory does not explain why the most plausible candidate for the title of 'labour aristocrats', the skilled metal workers, formed in all the main European industrial centres— Petrograd, Berlin, Turin, Sheffield, Glasgow—the vanguard of the great surge of working class revolt at the end of the First World War.[63] Secondly, contemporary versions of the theory, for example, the idea that Western workers benefit from 'unequal exchange' between North and South, focus on the fact that wage levels in the advanced countries are higher than those in the Third World. But the Marxist theory of exploitation (to which proponents of unequal exchange appeal) is not about absolute levels of impoverishment, but about the *relationship* between the wages workers receive, reflecting the value of their labour power, and the amount of surplus value they produce for the capitalists.

A highly paid worker may well be more exploited than a low paid worker because the former produces, relative to his wages, a larger amount of surplus value than the latter does. There is indeed reason to believe that the generally higher wages paid to Western workers reflect the greater costs of their reproduction; but the expenditure in particular on education and training which forms part of these costs creates a more highly skilled workforce which is therefore more productive and more exploited than its Third World counterparts.[64]

There is in any case a simple test of the proposition, essential to the labour aristocracy and unequal exchange theories, that Third World workers are more exploited than Western workers. If this were true, one would expect a constant flow of capital from the rich to the poor countries in search of the higher profits to be gained in the latter. In fact, according to the World Bank, between 1965 and 1983 two thirds of all foreign direct investment went to the advanced economies, and the rest to a handful of Newly Industrialising Countries (NICs). The debt crisis of the 1980s actually made the situation worse: capital flows from North to South almost dried up, while Third World capital flight and debt repayments meant there was, for much of the decade, a net transfer of financial resources from the poor to the rich countries.[65]

Writers such as Sivanandan are absolutely right to highlight and denounce the poverty and degradation to which imperialism condemns the masses of the Third World. But he relies on a doubly mistaken economic theory when he claims that 'the brunt of exploitation has shifted to the underdeveloped countries of the Third World', where 'capital does not need to pay peripheral labour a living wage to reproduce itself'.[66] This alleged development has passed Western capitalists by, who continue, as we have seen, to concentrate their investments in their own heartlands of Western Europe, North America and Japan. Moreover, while Sivanandan is right to point to the way in which capitalists in rich and poor countries alike often seek to increase their profits through extraction of absolute surplus value, based on reducing wages and lengthening working hours, he ignores the changes wrought by the partial industrialisation of the Third World. The emergence of the NICs of East Asia and Latin America has rested on the formation of relatively highly educated and skilled working classes which have in recent years been able to organise and to extract political and social reforms from their exploiters. The classic case is that of South Africa where, amid the appalling suffering and oppression caused by apartheid, the black working class has been able to build, in the shape of the Congress of South African Trade Unions, the most powerful labour movement in African history.[67] The bourgeoisie continues to create its own gravedigger in the shape of the working class. The new workers' movements of the Third World share a common interest with their Western brothers and sisters, black and white alike, in the overthrow of capitalism.

The fundamental reason why Marxists argue that racism is not in the interests of white workers is that, by dividing the working class, it weakens white as well as black workers. This proposition and the rival hypothesis that white workers gain from racism have been tested for the United States by the Marxist sociologist Al Szymanski. Szymanski sought to compare the situation of white and black workers in the 50 states of the Union. He found, first, that 'the higher black earnings relative to white, the higher white earnings relative to other whites' elsewhere in the US. This relationship—white workers were better off the narrower the gap between their wages and those of blacks—was stronger in states where at least 12 percent of the population were 'Third World' (ie black, Hispanic, Asian and native American), 'ie those states where economic discrimination against Third World people is able to have a significant economic effect on white earnings'. Szymanski found, secondly, that 'the higher the population of Third World people in a state's population, the *more* inequality there is among whites'. He concluded that 'the relatively poor white workers lose disproportionately from economic discrimination against Third World people compared with the better paid whites.' Thus 'white workers appear to actually lose economically from racial discrimination. These results appear to support the Marxist theory of the relationship between economic discrimination and white gain.' Szymanski found, thirdly, some evidence to support the hypothesis that 'the more intense racial discrimination is, the lower are the white earnings *because* of the intermediate variable of working-class solidarity—in other words, racism economically disadvantages white workers because it weakens trade union organisation by undermining the solidarity of black and white workers.'[68]

Szymanski's study suggests that racism is contrary to the interests of white workers, even when these interests are understood in the narrowest material terms. This is one facet of a much broader claim, namely that racism helps to keep capitalism going and thereby perpetuates the exploitation of white and black workers alike. White workers accept racist ideas not because it is in their interests to do so, but because of the way in which labour market competition among different groups of workers is worked up, by the conscious and unconscious efforts of the capitalists, into full scale racial divisions. At most what white workers receive is the imaginary solace of being members of the superior race, which helps to blind them to where their real interests lie. This analysis offers a cue to how the hold of racism on white workers can be broken—through the class struggles which pit them against the bosses and unite them with their black brothers and sisters.

Before, however, exploring this process, we must first consider another way in which black nationalists claim that black workers are materially set apart from their white fellows. This is the idea of a black 'underclass' advocated especially by Sivanandan. In fact, although he is very critical of the political conclusions drawn by *Marxism Today*, Sivanandan accepts its analysis of the emergence of a new 'post-Fordist' economy based on the destruction of the mass production industries and the working class these rested on. He merely argues that the effect of these changes is to shift the locus of resistance to the new 'underclass' which now bears the brunt of exploitation—'peripheral workers, home workers, *ad hoc* workers, casual, temporary, part-time workers—all the bits and pieces of the working class that the new productive forces have dispersed and dissipated their strength'.[69] This is, since Sivanandan, unlike Martin Jacques, Stuart Hall and the other theorists of 'New Times', still wants to fight capitalism, a remarkably pessimistic analysis. It is, however, a completely mistaken one. As I have shown elsewhere, the whole idea of a new 'post-Fordist' phase of 'flexible accumulation' which no longer rests on mass industrial production is completely untenable.[70]

Ideas of an underclass in particular involve a gross exaggeration of limited trends. Thus the proportion of the employed and self employed working part time rose in Britain from 21 percent in 1984 to 22 percent in 1991 (the proportion of women working part time actually fell slightly in the same period). The proportion of those in temporary jobs was 5.7 percent in 1984, 5.8 percent in 1991.[71] Moreover, the concept of the underclass is wholly misleading in suggesting that black people typically occupy a marginal economic position in the advanced countries.

*TABLE: UNEMPLOYMENT RATES BY ETHNIC ORIGIN AND SEX
GREAT BRITAIN, SPRING 1991 (%)*

	All persons	Men	Women
All persons of working age	8.3	9.1	7.3
Whites	8	9	7
Ethnic minority groups	15	16	14
of which:			
West Indian/Guyanese	15	18	12
Indian	12	12	11
Pakistani/Bangladeshi	25	25	24
All other ethnic origins	14	14	14

*Source: M Naylor and E Purdie, 'Results of the 1991 Labour Force Survey',
Employment Gazette, April 1992, Table 20*

An ambitious Marxist survey of contemporary class structure, conducted in the United States in 1980 under the supervision of Erik Olin Wright, found that no less than 74.5 percent of blacks were workers, as opposed to 49.7 percent of whites. Interestingly, it found that 15.4 percent of all blacks and 21.4 percent of black men were skilled workers (the equivalent figure for all whites was 12.4 percent and for white men 16.7 percent.)[72] No comparably rigorous study has been made of the British class structure, but the unemployment figures in the 1991 Labour Force Survey (see table) are indicative. The average rate of unemployment among blacks is 15 percent, almost twice that among whites (8 percent). This is clear evidence of the effects of racism: blacks are more likely than whites to suffer unemployment. Nevertheless the overwhelming majority of blacks are in employment, as wage labourers, part of the same working class as their white brothers and sisters.

Racism and the class struggle

These are arguments about the material situation and interests of black and white workers. Black nationalists tend to see the black community as the chief agent of the struggle against racism. For Sivanandan it is the 'communities of resistance' forged by the black 'underclass' out of struggle which bear the main burden of fighting capital today.[73] Culture is accorded a central role in the creation of such communities. Paul Gilroy argues that 'collective identities, spoken through "race", community and locality are, for all their spontaneity, powerful means to coordinate action and create solidarity. The constructed "traditional" culture becomes a means…to articulate personal autonomy with collective empowerment'.[74]

This stress on culture is far from wholly mistaken. The attempts, for example, to develop an 'Afrocentric' history which recovers the achievements of precolonial African societies and the centuries of heroic struggle by black people against Western imperialism and racism can be an important source of black pride infusing contemporary political movements with strength: the real value of Cedric Robinson's *Black Marxism*, for example, lies in the contribution it makes to this process of recovery. But to base the struggle against racism on the idea of a black community united by a culture of resistance carries with it great dangers. Probably the most obvious is that blacks form a minority of the population in the advanced capitalist countries—10 percent in the US, 5 percent in Britain. Central to the defeat of the greatest and most heroic of all black nationalist movements, the Black Power movement which emerged in the US from the great ghetto risings of the 1960s, was the failure of even its most advanced wing, represented by Malcolm X and the Black Panthers, to link the struggle for black liberation with that of white workers against their exploitation. This allowed the ruling class to isolate and ultimately to destroy the black radicals, many of whose best leaders were murdered or jailed.[75]

A strategic focus on the black *community*, secondly, conceals the class antagonisms within this 'community'. Again the US provides the best illustration. Manning Marable, himself an influential black radical theorist, observes: 'The net result of affirmative action and civil rights initiatives was to expand the potential base of the African-American middle class... By 1989, one out of seven African-American families had incomes exceeding 50,000 dollars annually, compared to less than 22,000 dollars for the average black household.' The process of class differentiation among blacks underlies the rise of the black politicians who now largely manage America's cities. Marable confesses: 'Most of us have not anticipated an ideological shift among many African-American or Latino politicians, using racial solidarity to ensure minority voter loyalty, but gradually embracing more moderate to conservative public policy positions, especially on economic issues.'[76] Black politicians have become the district commissioners of a ruling class that is still predominantly white, defending a racist system against the very people who elected them. I write these lines as downtown Los Angeles burns after the acquittal of the four white policemen videotaped beating up Ronald King. What difference to those protesting does it make that a black mayor and soon a black police chief preside over LA's racist power structure?

Thirdly, theorists like Gilroy who place the main emphasis on the development of a culture of resistance ignore the way in which culture can divide, rather than unite, black people. The recovery of, or return to, a tradition may appeal only to particular groups of black people. Many Asians, for example, may feel that Afrocentric history has nothing to offer them. The renewed interest in Islam among many young British Asians may cut them off from many other black people, let alone from white workers. The Newham Monitoring Project and the Campaign against Racism and Fascism make a relevant point when discussing the anti-racist policies of the Greater London Council and other left Labour led London councils in the early 1980s:

Instead of welding those groups previously excluded from the local state to form a movement for socialism, local authority funding policies actually placed the groups in a competitive relationship with each other. In the black community, this accentuated the differences between Asians, Africans and Caribbeans, and even divided the groups among themselves. Over the previ-

ous decade at least, there had been a significant political dimension to black struggles, but council funding tended to promote the more cultural and less political organisations. Furthermore, the focus on 'ethnicity' within council funding policy tended to promote religious and cultural organisations over campaigning ones.[77]

These tensions are one example of the rise of what is sometimes called 'identity politics' in the 1980s. In the absence of large scale struggles against oppression, the oppressed themselves tended to fragment into smaller groups, each tending to highlight their different 'identities', the particularity of *their* oppression compared to those of others—blacks of African origin versus Asians, black women versus gentile white women versus Jewish white women, gays versus lesbians versus bisexuals. This kind of fragmentation can only weaken any real struggle against the system which produces all the different forms of oppression. Of course, appeals to culture need not have this kind of effect. Real cultures of resistance can be forged which include and unite rather than exclude and divide. But then why should such a culture be confined to black people? Why shouldn't it unite blacks and whites in a common struggle in the way in which Rock Against Racism sought to in the late 1970s? Indeed, Mike Davis, who calls the Los Angeles rising the 'first modern multi-ethnic riot' in the US, argues that rap has helped to create 'a broad interface between black youth culture and Latino youth culture' in Los Angeles.[78]

Any such non-racial culture of resistance can invoke a history largely ignored by black radicals, that of working class struggles which brought together blacks and whites. One of the great achievements of Peter Fryer's superb and moving history of black people in Britain is its reconstruction of the role played by black radicals such as the Spencean William Davidson and the Chartist William Cuffay in the great revolutionary workers' movements of the early 19th century. Their participation in these struggles reflects the fact that the demand for the abolition of slavery in the British Empire, finally achieved in the 1830s, had as its main source of mass support the working class radicals who linked the struggle for black emancipation to that against oligarchy in Britain itself.[79] Nor is it the case that the final defeat of Chartism at the end of the 1840s marked a decisive break in this tradition, signalling the growing incorporation of at least a layer of workers in imperialism.[80] To take a much more recent case, the inner city riots of 1981 represent the closest British parallel to the great American ghetto risings of the 1960s. Yet, as Chris Harman noted at the time, though the British riots were sparked off usually by police racism, in '*virtually all*' of them 'there has been significant white involvement alongside blacks, and the involvement has not just been of white leftists, but of white working-class youth.'[81] Of those arrested in the riots, 67 percent were white, 20 percent West Indians and Africans, 5 percent Asians.[81] These were *class* riots, bringing together black and white youth rebelling against a common experience of unemployment as well as specific issues, notably policy harassment, which particularly affected blacks. In this respect at least the Los Angeles rebellion resembles the British riots more closely than Watts or Detroit.

Examples of this can be multiplied. Even in the US at the height of Jim Crow in the late 19th and early 20th centuries, each great surge of mass workers' organisation, whether it was the Knights of Labor in the 1880s, the American Federation of Labor in the early 1890s, or the International Workers of the World in the years before 1914, brought together black and white workers across the racial barriers.[83] The importance of these examples of inter-racial working class unity is, even if they were sometimes short lived, that they show that the level of class struggle is the decisive factor in determining the intensity of racism. Generally speaking, the higher the level of class struggle, the greater workers' militancy, confidence and self organisation, the wider the layers of the class involved in any particular movement, the weaker the hold of racism on them.

The London dockers are a case in point. Notoriously in April 1968 they went on strike for a day and marched on the Houses of Parliament in support of Enoch Powell's 'rivers of blood' speech calling for an end to black immigration. The dockers' action reflected the rundown of their industry under a Labour government which did nothing to defend their interests. In despair and anger they looked to Powell instead. By contrast, in July 1972 the dockers, relying now on their own shop stewards' organisation, inflicted a decisive defeat on the Tory Industrial Relations Act when they forced the release of the Pentonville Five. The confidence this victory instilled in the dockers strengthened support for more generalised class politics. Five years later, on 11 July 1977, the Royal Docks Shop Stewards banner headed a mass picket of 5,000 overwhelmingly white trade unionists in support of the predominantly Asian workforce at Grunwicks in west London. The London dockers were largely resistant to the surge of fascism which swept Britain in the late 1970s.

There is, this example suggests, an inverse relationship between the level of class struggle and the intensity of racism. The crucial factor underlying this relationship is workers' self confidence. When the class is engaging successfully in battles with the bosses, then white workers are more likely to place their confidence in workers' self organisation to defend their interests, and to see themselves as part of the same class as their black brothers and sisters. By contrast, when the workers' movement is on the defensive and the employers are generally able to impose their will, then workers are much less likely to look towards class based collective organisation and action to solve their problems. Racism can, in these circumstances, increase its hold on white workers, both because of the psychological compensations it seems to promise, and because it offers a diagnosis of their situation that focuses their resentments on a visible scapegoat, black people.

This analysis can be illustrated by an interesting study of Newham in east London by the Newham Monitoring Project and the Campaign against Racism and Fascism. It documents the growth of racism in the borough during the 1970s. In the October 1974 general election the main Nazi group, the National Front, won the votes of 5,000 Newham residents, the largest NF vote in the country. According to a leading black activist in the area, Unmesh Desai, in 1980, 'anywhere east of Liverpool Street—and this is very difficult for people to comprehend now—was regarded as a no go area for black people.' The spread of racism in Newham took place against the background of the rundown of local industry—between 1966 and 1972, 45 percent of the 40,000 jobs in Canning Town were lost and only one in three replaced—and the failure of the Labour Party, which controlled the borough council, to offer any effective alternative:

Newham, by the mid-1970s, had become one of the most neglected and deprived areas in the country. According to New Society (23 October 1975), it had the largest number of houses without bath or inside lavatory in London; the highest perinatal mortality rate (that is, stillbirths and deaths in the first week) and the highest percentage of mentally ill in the country. Only one in 40 schoolchildren went to university (the national figure was three times as high) and only one in ten received any form of further education (the national figure was almost one in four)... The general poverty and decline were aggravated by the way power was concentrated in the hands of a few individual councillors and council officers sought to manage social problems (and no more so than in the area of housing) by playing one group off against another.[84]

Leading Labour Party members indeed expressed openly racist attitudes: 'at a local Labour Party ward meeting, the former mayor of Newham (a local magistrate) started talking about the "coons", how they smelt, how he couldn't stand the smell of their cooking and how, if he had his own way, he would send them all back to where they came from.' It was in this climate that 'a substantial section of the white working class turned its electoral support away from the Labour Party to the NF. The latter might not be able to provide new houses and jobs or to alleviate the material conditions, but its message of white pride spoke to a psychological need.'[85]

Newham in the 1970s illustrates on a micro scale the process involved in the rise of the National Front in France during the 1980s. There a social democratic government presided over levels of unemployment higher over the decade than those in Thatcherite Britain and responded to the growth of racism by tightening up immigration restrictions; it is hardly surprising that millions of disillusioned working class voters deserted the parties of the reformist left, the Socialists and Communists, for Jean Marie Le Pen. These examples highlight the fact that rises in the level of racism are not, as is sometimes believed, an automatic consequence of deteriorating economic conditions. Working class people's experience of economic crisis is mediated by the role played by their political and industrial organisations. The failure of reformist organisations to mount an effective struggle against rising unemployment and falling living standards is often critical in laying workers open to racist ideas.

The subjective factor, the conscious attempt by political organisations to influence the course of history, can also play a decisive role in combating the spread of racism. The divergent experiences of Britain and France in the 1980s bear this out. The Newham study (published in 1991) reports: 'Ten years ago, Asian and Afro-Caribbean people across the whole of Newham, both north and south, were experiencing similar levels of racial harassment. But throughout the 1980s, a series of self-defence campaigns radically altered the climate in the north.' The study, while stressing the importance of the defence campaigns initiated by black people themselves—for example, after the 1980 murder of Akhtar Ali Baig by fascist skinheads—also acknowledges the role played by white anti-racists, for example, of the Labour left wingers who were able to reverse some of the council's most obnoxious racist practices (such as demanding that black people produce passports before their housing applications could be considered) and were responsible for Newham in 1984 becoming the first local authority to evict a white family for racial harassment. Reflecting on the experience of the Newham Monitoring Project, Unmesh Desai noted:

> *another lesson we learned in those early days was that it was not white individuals who were the problem but white society as a whole. Anti-racism has also to speak to the problems of the white working class, who we have to live cheek by jowl with, and can't get away from.*[86]

These developments in Newham were part of a nationwide process, one of whose main features was the precipitate decline of the NF and other fascist organisations at the end of the 1970s. This serious defeat for the far right in Britain was a direct consequence of the emergence of a mass anti-fascist movement, the Anti Nazi League, launched by the Socialist Workers Party and Labour left wingers in 1978. Yet the ANL has often been attacked by black nationalists. Paul Gilroy, for example, claims that 'the ANL deliberately sought to summon and manipulate a form of nationalism and patriotism as part of its broad anti-fascist drive', concentrating in its propaganda on the charge that 'the British Nazis were merely sham patriots'. Moreover, 'being "Anti Nazi" located the problem posed by the growth of racism in Britain exclusively at the level of a small and eccentric, though violent, band of neo-fascists.'[87] This indictment can be contested at a number of levels. In the first place, ANL propaganda focused, not on the Nazis' lack of patriotism, but on the fact that they were *Nazis*, active supporters of a political ideology which had led to the Holocaust. If there was a historical image to which the ANL appealed, it wasn't Britain's 'Finest Hour' in 1940, as Gilroy contends, but Auschwitz: hence its main slogan, 'Never again!'

At the same time, the ANL was based on a united front of social democrats and revolutionary socialists with differing analyses of racism and strategies of change. Labour ANL supporters, given their general commitment to British nationalism, did sometimes attack the Nazis' lack of patriotism. We in the SWP certainly did not. Nor did we isolate the struggle against fascism from broader questions of racism. For example, at the first ANL carnival in May 1978 an SWP pamphlet called *The Case against Immigration Controls* sold heavily; the ANL conference in 1979 passed a resolution proposed by the SWP which rejected immigration controls. It is of the nature of a united front that it brings together divergent political forces which are prepared to work together around a single issue, in this case combating the Nazis. Focusing in this way on the fascists wasn't a retreat from the more general struggle against racism; on the contrary, it was essential to the conduct of that struggle at the time. The growth of the NF and other Nazi organisations of course reflected a much more deep seated racism institutionalised in British society and pandered to by the main parties. But the rise of the NF (who one commentator predicted, in 1977, would soon overtake the Liberals as the third main party),[88] if unhindered, would have promoted a qualitative increase in the level of racism, allowing the Nazis to entrench themselves in many working class areas where they could draw on white popular support to attack black people with impunity and demand the implementation of even more racist policies by local authorities and central government. We can see this dynamic at work in France, where the official racism of the state and the main bourgeois parties feeds off and also reinforces the popular racism stoked up by the Nazis. The ANL, by targeting and mobilising against the Nazis, stopped this dynamic in its tracks, and thereby helped to prevent a further intensification in the level of racism.[89]

The defeat inflicted on British fascism at the end of the 1970s is no reason for complacency. Racism is inherent in capitalist society, and the conditions promoting it are constantly being recreated by the system's crisis. But the contrast between the British case and that of France since 1981 is instructive. It suggests that the failure of the French far left—which includes a number of sizeable and long established organisations—to build an anti-fascist movement comparable to the ANL is a major factor in the growth of the National Front. This in turn highlights the role which revolutionary socialists can play in the struggle against racism. They can do so at two levels. First, revolutionaries should be involved in the battles which develop around different aspects of racism—not just (or often primarily) against the Nazis, but against tighter immigration restrictions, attacks like the current one on the right of asylum, the deportations of individuals, police brutality, racial attacks. This active commitment to the struggle against racism in all its aspects includes support for black people when they organise against their oppression and when they take their grievances onto the streets, to challenge the racist state.

Secondly, however, revolutionary socialists are also committed to building a non-racist party of black and white workers which understands that racism can only be finally removed through the overthrow of the capitalist system. This strategy does not imply telling black people to wait for the socialist revolution. As we have seen, revolutionaries involve themselves fully in the daily battles against racism. But they do so understanding, not simply that racism has its roots in capitalism, but that capitalism itself can only be overthrown by a working class that has overcome its racial divisions and united against the common enemy. Revolutionary socialists are anti-racists not only because they despise racism for the moral obscenity that it is, but because a working class movement which does not confront racism will not be able to overthrow capital. The working class, as we have seen, is an international class: the spread of capitalism across the globe has created a proletariat that is itself spread across the globe and which has been formed by large scale immigration across national borders. Breaking down the racial barriers which this process helps erect between different groups of workers is a necessary condition of any successful socialist revolution.

From this perspective we can see why the charges that Marxism is 'Eurocentric' made by black radicals such as Cedric Robinson are mistaken. Marxism indeed emerged in Western Europe in response to the appearance of industrial capitalism, the capitalist mode of production in its developed form. At the centre of Marx's theory was his analysis of this unprecedented phenomenon. In the *Communist Manifesto* and the *Grundrisse* in particular he stresses capitalism's *universalising* role, the way in which it dragged humankind willy nilly into the first genuinely global social system in history. Marx was clear sighted about the terrible suffering this entailed, especially for the peoples of what we now call the Third World: 'the extirpation, enslavement and entombment in mines of the indigenous population [of America]..., the beginnings of the conquest and plunder of India, and the conversion of Africa into a preserve for the commercial hunting of black skins are all things which characterise the dawn of the era of capitalist production.'[90] But Marx argued that the emergence of the capitalist world system created the conditions of what he called 'human emancipation'—a revolution which in overthrowing capitalism would lay the basis of the abolition of class exploitation altogether and of all the other forms of oppression dividing and disabling humankind. Such a comprehensive emancipation was possible because capitalism rested on a universal class, the proletariat, a world class, formed from all the peoples of the globe, which could liberate itself only through an international revolution founded on the common interests of the exploited.

This conception of human emancipation informs the politics of the revolutionary Marxist tradition. It explains why, for example, the Communist International was, in the years immediately after the Russian Revolution of October 1917, the first socialist movement to see itself as a genuinely global movement which linked the struggle of the industrial working class to the anti-imperialist revolt of the colonial masses, whom Lenin and the Bolsheviks conceived as the subject of their own emancipation. It was the same vision of human emancipation which led CLR James to rally to the revolutionary socialist tradition—a commitment from which, whatever the peculiarities of his understanding of the tradition, he never thereafter flinched—and which kept other radical black intellectuals like WEB Du Bois in a creative dialogue with Marxism. Even a version of this vision which had been debased by Stalinism allowed the Communist Party of the USA to build a significant base in Harlem during the 1930s (and to have an important influence on the riot of March 1935), despite fierce competition from black nationalists, notably followers of Marcus Garvey, and on the basis of an intransigent defence of the class unity of black and white workers.[92] The great rebellions of black people, from the Haitian Revolution to the ghetto risings—and now the Los Angeles riots—are part of the revolutionary tradition which seeks to unite the movements for socialism and for black liberation. The struggle against racial oppression is an indispensable part of the revolutionary socialist project. Equally, however, without that project, the fight against racism cannot finally be won.

Notes
I am grateful to Lindsey German, Chris Harman, Kevin Ovenden and John Rees for their help in the writing of this article. Peter Alexander's *Racism, Resistance and Revolution* (London, 1987) provided a starting point for many of its themes.

1   See A Sivanandan, *Communities of Resistance* (London, 1990), ch 4, for a devastating critique of RAT.
2   An early example of 'social-cultural pluralism' is Dilip Hiro's influential *Black British White British* (first published 1971: rev edn, London, 1992). In this article I use the term 'black' to refer to all those who are racially oppressed on the grounds of their colour. Blackness is thus a political rather than a biological or cultural concept. It is hard to overstate the stupidity of those who, under the influence of 'identity politics', seek to differentiate among groups of black people in order to pick out one (usually those of African origin) as more oppressed than another (typically those of Asian origin).
3   For a brief statement of the Marxist case, see A Callinicos, *The Fight against Racism* (London, 1992).
4   A Sivanandan, 'All that Melts into Air is Solid', reprinted in *Communities*.
5   C Robinson, *Black Marxism* (London, 1983), pp2-3, 3-5.
6   Ibid, pp451, 244. Another radical black intellectual, Cornel West, is much more open in espousing essentially religious beliefs—what he calls 'Christian prophetic pragmatism': see *The American Evasion of Philosophy* (London, 1989), ch 6.
7   C Robinson, *Black Marxism*, op cit, p82.
8   M Marable, *How Capitalism Underdeveloped Black America* (Boston, 1983), p260.
9   P Fryer, *Staying Power* (London, 1984), pp165-190.
10 S Rose et al, *Not in Our Genes* (Harmondsworth, 1984), pp126-127.
11 J Herrin, *The Formation of Christendom* (Oxford, 1987), p8.
12 H Arendt, *The Origins of Totalitarianism* (London, 1986), p7.
13 A Bauman, *Modernity and the Holocaust* (Cambridge, 1991), p35. The tensions surrounding the Jews' position in pre-modern Europe were, in fact, closely related to their peculiar economic role as often the main practitioners of commerce in predominantly agrarian societies: see A Leon, *The Jewish Question* (New York, 1970), esp. chs III and IV.
14 H Arendt, *Origins*, p87.
15 The following draws on A Callinicos, 'A Note on Racism in the Ancient World', *International Socialism* 2:37 (1988).
16 A Bauman, *Modernity*, pp62-63, 65.
17 F M Snowden Jnr, *Blacks in Antiquity* (Cambridge, Mass, 1970), pp182-183.
18 M Bernal, *Black Athena*, I (London, 1991), pp1-2.
19 O Murray, *Archaic Greece* (London, 1980).
20 See P Anderson, *Passages from Antiquity to Feudalism* (London, 1974), GEM de Ste Croix, *The Class Struggle in the Ancient Greek World* (London, 1981), and EM Wood, *Peasant-Citizen and Slave* (London, 1988).
21 M Bernal, *Black Athena*, p1.
22 Herodotus, *The Histories*, Bk. II.
23 A Momigliano, *Alien Wisdom* (Cambridge, 1975), p131.
24 P Fryer, *Staying Power*, op cit, p134.
25 D Hume, *Essays, Moral, Political, and Literary* (Indianapolis, 1985), pp629-630. Hume slightly toned down the racism of this passage in its final version: see ibid, p208 n10.
26 R Blackburn, *The Overthrow of Colonial Slavery 1776-1848* (London, 1988), Introduction.

27 E Williams, *Capitalism and Slavery* (New York, 1961), p6.
28 R Blackburn, *Overthrow*, op cit, p11.
29 B J Fields, 'Slavery, Race and Ideology in the United States of America', *New Left Review*, 181 (1990), p102.
30 Ibid, pp102-3.
31 Ibid, p105.
32 EM Wood, 'Capitalism and Human Emancipation', *New Left Review*, 167 (1988), p7.
33 Marx, *Capital*, I (Harmondsworth, 1976), p899; *Capital*, III (Moscow, 1971), pp790-792.
34 I Khaldûn, *The Muquaddimah* (3 vols, New-York, 1958), I, pp80-81.
35 Marx, *Grundrisse* (Harmondsworth, 1973), p507.
36 Marx, *Capital*, I pp279-280.
37 B J Fields, 'Slavery', op cit, p114.
38 P Fryer, *Staying Power*, op cit, p134.
39 See Hitchens' interesting discussion of Kipling's role as the 'Bard of Empire' in *Blood, Class and Nostalgia* (London, 1990), ch. 3.
40 P Fryer, *Staying Power*, op cit, p190.
41 M Barker, *The New Racism* (London, 1981). See also, for example, P Gilroy, *'There Ain't No Black in the Union Jack'* (London, 1987), ch 2.
42 See S Rose et al, *Not in Our Genes*, op cit, for criticisms of these and related ideas.
43 A striking example is D Hiro's discussion of Afro-Caribbeans: see *Black British*, op cit, pp22-25.
44 The South African Marxist Neville Alexander develops an important critique of the concept of ethnicity in his book (written under the pseudonym No Sizwe) *One Azania, One Nation* (London, 1979).
45 E J Hobsbawm, *The Age of Capital 1848-1875* (London, 1977), p228; see generally ibid, ch 11.
46 See S Castles and G Kosack, *Immigrant Workers and Class Structure in Western Europe* (London, 1973).
47 See J Rollo, 'Immigrant Workers in Western Europe', II, *International Socialism*, 97 (Old Series, 1977).
48 Marx and Engels, *Selected Correspondence* (Moscow, 1965), pp236-237.
49 See M Davis, *Prisoners of the American Dream* (London, 1986), ch 1.
50 P Foner, *Organized Labour and the Black Worker 1619-1981* (New York, 1981), ch 1. There are in fact further complications in the relationship between economic competition and racial divisions. For one thing, the economic and ethnic differences between groups of workers don't necessarily harden into full-scale racial antagonisms: in the US, for example, the black-white divide has usually overridden other tensions, for example, those among whites of different national and religious backgrounds. For another, the economic tensions don't have to be between different groups of workers: consider, for example, the conflicts that have developed between Korean shopkeepers and the black poor in a number of major American cities, and which were involved in the Los Angeles riots at the end of April 1992.
51 WEB Du Bois, *Black Reconstruction in America 1860-1880* (New York, 1969), pp700-701.
52 See James's correspondence with Martin Glaberman, in P Buhle (ed), *C L R James: His Life and Work* (London, 1988), pp153-163.
53 Marx and Engels, *Collected Works*, III (London, 1975), p175.
54 B Anderson, *Imagined Communities* (London, 1983), pp15-16, 136.
55 P Gilroy, *'Ain't No Black'*, op cit, pp44ff.
56 E J Hobsbawm, *The Age of Empire 1875-1914* (London, 1987), chs 5 and 6.
57 See EO Wright et al, *Reconstructing Marxism* (London, 1992), pp63-67, for a useful critique of the idea, put about by sociologists like Anthony Giddens, that explaining

racism by the 'beneficial effects for capitalism' it has because of 'its consequences for working-class disunity (divide and conquer)' is an untenable piece of 'functionalism'.

58 C Robinson, *Black Marxism*, op cit, p451.
59 P Gilroy, *'Ain't No Black'*, op cit, pp23-24.
60 A Sivanandan, *Communities*, op cit, p52.
61 See the quotations from WEB Du Bois' 'The African Roots of War' (1915) in C Robinson, *Black Marxism*, op cit, pp334-335, n72.
62 R Ramdin, *The Making of the Black Working Class in Britain* (Aldershot, 1987), p63.
63 See, for example, T Cliff, 'The Economic Roots of Reformism', in *Neither Washington nor Moscow* (London, 1992).
64 See M Kidron, 'Black Reformism', in *Capitalism and Theory* (London, 1974).
65 A Callinicos, 'Marxism and Imperialism Today', *International Socialism*, 2:50 (1991), pp19-25.
66 A Sivanandan, *Communities*, op cit, p181.
67 See J Baskin, *Striking Back* (Johannesburg, 1991).
68 A Szymanski, 'Racial Discrimination and White Gain', *American Sociological Review*, 41 (1976), pp409-412.
69 A Sivanandan, *Communities*, p29.
70 A Callinicos, *Against Postmodernism* (Cambridge, 1989), ch 5.
71 M Naylor and E Purdie, 'Results of the 1991 Labour Force Survey', *Employment Gazette*, April 1992, Tables 6 and 9.
72 EO Wright, *Classes* (London, 1985), Table 6.4, p201. These figures should be taken as only indicative, since, because of flaws in Wright's theory of classes, they almost certainly understate the size of the working class. See A Callinicos and C Harman, *The Changing Working Class* (London, 1987), Appendix.
73 A Sivanandan, *Communities*, op cit, pp51-58.
74 P Gilroy, *'Ain't No Black'* op cit, p247.
75 See A Shawki, 'Black Liberation and Socialism in the United States', *International Socialism*, 2:47 (1990).
76 Quoted in S Smith, 'Twilight of the American Dream', *International Socialism*, 2:54 (1992), pp20, 22.
77 *Forging a Black Community: Asian and Afro-Caribbean Struggles in Newham* (London, 1991), p47.
78 Interview in *Socialist Review*, June 1992.
79 P Fryer, *Staying Power*, op cit, pp203-246.
80 See J Foster, *Class Struggle and the Industrial Revolution* (London, 1977).
81 C Harman, 'The Summer of 1981: A Post-Riot Analysis', *International Socialism*, 2:14 (1981), p14.
82 D Hiro, *Black British*, op cit, p90.
83 P Foner, *Organized Labor*, op cit, chs 4-6.
84 *Forging a Black Community*, op cit, pp12, 28, 31, 41.
85 Ibid, 32.
86 Ibid, pp1, 48.
87 P Gilroy, *'Ain't No Black'*, op cit, pp131, 133.
88 M Walker, *The National Front* (London, 1977).
89 See, more generally, C Bambery, *Killing the Nazi Menace* (London, 1992). It is sometimes claimed that it was not the ANL, but rather Thatcher, with her appeal to white fears of being 'swamped by people with a different culture', who killed off the Nazis, by stealing their clothes. This isn't a specially plausible explanation. For one thing, the Tories were relatively cautious about mounting any full scale offensive against black people after 1979, and especially after the 1981 riots (only in the last couple of years have there been signs of the Tories wishing to make serious use of race and immigration as issues). In any case, as the French case discussed in the text

shows, official racism tends to *strengthen* the fascists by giving them confidence and their ideas greater legitimacy. This certainly was the pattern in Britain in the 1960s and 1970s: see, for example, P Foot, *Immigration and Race in British Politics* (Harmondsworth, 1965).

90 Marx, *Capital*, I, op cit, p915.
91 See A Callinicos, *Trotskyism* (Milton Keynes, 1990), pp61-66, and A Shawki, 'Black Liberation', op cit, pp58-68.
92 M Naison, *Communists in Harlem during the Depression* (New York, 1983), esp pt I.

Racism and class struggle in the American Civil War era

A review of Iver Bernstein, **The New York City Draft Riots: Their Significance for American Society and Politics in the Age of the Civil War** *(Oxford University Press, 1990) £24*

LEE SUSTAR

Introduction

The civil war in the United States began 'as a war in the interest of slavery on both sides', as the greatest abolitionist, the escaped slave Frederick Douglass put it. 'The South was fighting to take slavery out of the Union, and the North was fighting to keep it in the Union...'[1]

Douglass grasped the contradictions of what Alex Callinicos calls a 'bourgeois revolution from above'.[2] But revolution it was. Despite the Union's reluctance to overthrow slavery, black emancipation proved necessary for the North to win what Karl Marx termed 'nothing but a struggle between two social systems, between the system of slavery and the system of free labour'.[3] The freeing of four million black slaves not only destroyed the slave owning class but detonated a massive confrontation between labour and capital that dwarfed antebellum class struggle.

The smashing of the slave power—the completion of the bourgeois revolution begun in 1776—led directly to a showdown between labour and capital. As Marx observed:

In the United States of America, every independent movement of the workers was paralysed so long as slavery disfigured a part of the Republic. Labour cannot emancipate itself in the white skin where in the black it is branded. But out of the death of slavery a new life at once arose. The first fruit of the civil war was the eight hours agitation, that ran with the seven-leagued boots of the locomotive from the Atlantic to the Pacific.[4]

The 'new life' that excited Marx would be difficult. Not only would it take decades to secure the eight hour day, but racism would continue to distort and weaken the organised labour movement in the US. The 1877 reconciliation of Northern industrialists with the deposed ex-slaveholding class overthrew the radical bourgeois democracy of Reconstruction and ushered in a half century of political reaction in which white supremacy held sway—North as well as South. This, coupled with a series of decisive industrial defeats for workers, eventually allowed the ex-slaveholders' party—the Democrats—to reconstitute their antebellum role as 'the workingmen's party' in the North.

The eventual dominance of white supremacy in the US labour movement is usually seen by historians as inevitable. Rather than examine the tremendous extent to which white and black workers forged inter-racial unity in the revolutionary aftermath of the civil war, historians have tended to stress the apparent continuity between antebellum racial attitudes and white workers' racism today.[5] In this view, the dominance of the Democratic Party in the labour movement was in large part the political expression of white workers' preference for alliances with white employers rather than workplace solidarity with black or immigrant workers. As Ahmed Shawki puts it:

Such interpretations of the civil war and Reconstruction downplay the significance of these events, and crucially the possibility of any outcome other than that which occurred. But the importance of this period is precisely that it showed that racism was not immutable and that ideas can change rapidly in periods of social upheaval... The civil war destroyed slavery in the South, but it did not establish a new political and economic order in its place. The next three decades witnessed an intense, often violent, political struggle to determine the character of the South. In the end, white supremacy was re-established, but it was not a foregone conclusion.[6]

Iver Bernstein's *The New York City Draft Riots* isolates a pivotal moment in that period. By examining in detail an extreme example of racist violence in the American working class, Bernstein highlights the speed and scope of the qualitative changes in working class consciousness and organisation brought about by the civil war.

Although the draft riots featured some of the most horrific anti-black violence in US history, they simultaneously represented a growing class polarisation that would undermine the Democrats' working class base. Bernstein explains how, just a few years after the anti-black pogroms, workers in New York launched a struggle for the eight hour day—a struggle that included black workers. Politically, the eight hour movement was dominated by the Radical Republicans in much of the country. But Bernstein's detailed study of class struggle in New York shows why workers asserted their independence from both Republicans and Democrats to create some of the first significant socialist activity in the US labour movement. In particular, Bernstein exposes the contradictions in the Democratic Party's role as mediating structure between (white) labour and capital.

More generally, *The New York City Draft Riots* provides an excellent vantage point from which to view the astonishingly resilient struggle for inter-racial labour solidarity in three decades following the civil war. In so doing, the book deepens our understanding of racism in the American working class and the potential for overcoming it.

Labour, anti-slavery and the Republican Party

By the time of the civil war most Northern workers were opposed to slavery. But opposition to slavery was not the same as being for the abolition of slavery. The main slogans of the Republican Party, 'Free Soil, Free Labour', united a disparate coalition of ex-Democrats and Whigs on the basis of opposition to the *extension* of slavery, not its overthrow. Nevertheless, abolitionism did find a large audience in the labour movement. Although the leadership of the abolitionist movement were thoroughly middle class, the most radical among them developed a critique of capitalism and tried to build links to the working class. For example, the Massachusetts Anti-Slavery Society adopted this resolution in 1849:

> *Whereas the rights of the labourer at the North are identical with those of the Southern slave, and cannot be obtained as long as chattel slavery rears its hydra head in our land... [Resolved] That it is equally incumbent upon the working men of the North to espouse the cause of emancipation of the slave and upon abolitionists to advocate the claims of the free labourer.*[7]

The frequent anti-abolitionist riots in Northern cities were not, as some historians claim, spontaneous pro-slavery demonstrations by workers. They were highly organised by businessmen, politicians and journalists connected to slavery via economic interests and the Democratic Party. In upstate New York in 1835 an anti-abolition riot was led by a member of the US Congress who would go on to become the state's attorney general and chief justice. The bloody 1836 anti-abolitionist riot in Cincinnati was joined by the city's mayor, a bank president and a former US senator. After sacking an abolitionist newspaper the mob attacked the city's black neighbourhoods. In Boston well known merchants and politicians participated in the anti-abolition riots. In late 1860, on the eve of the civil war, a *Chicago Times* editorial whipped up a racism by denouncing the 'hideous monster, Abolition', and concluded: 'Abolition is disunion. It is the Alpha and Omega of our National woes—*strangle it*.'[8]

Despite this steady stream of pro-slavery propaganda and organised violence, substantial sections of the Northern working class were attracted to abolitionism. One militant abolitionist noted in his memoirs that 'the anti-slavery movement was…primarily a people's movement…far stronger for a time in the factories and the shoe shops than in the pulpits and colleges.' A study of those who signed abolitionist petitions in New England and New York industrial towns found that most were artisans and workers.[9] As historian Eric Foner noted, 'The central values of the early labour movement—liberty, democracy, personal independence, the right of the worker to the fruits of his or her labour—were obviously incompatible with the institution of slavery.'[10]

The connections between the abolitionists and the labour movement foreshadowed the alliance of organised labour with the Radical Republicans during Reconstruction in the struggle for the eight hour day. Ultimately Radical Republicanism collapsed in the 1870s in an intensifying clash between the two key 'producing classes'—workers and capitalists.

But in New York City the Republican cross class alliance was a nonstarter. With its disproportionate concentrations of labour and capital and rapid pace of industrialisation, the class struggle was far sharper than anywhere else in the US.[11] Moreover, the small farmers who made up the middle class backbone of the Republican Party in the rest of the US were socially insignificant in New York City. The result was that the explosive class conflicts of the civil war and Reconstruction put the New York City working class on a political trajectory away from both Republicans and Democrats, towards independent labour politics and socialism.

Antebellum class struggle in New York

The decade before the civil war saw unprecedented economic growth in New York, the largest city in the US and then the nation's centre of heavy industry. But there was a tremendous increase in social tensions. Twenty two workers were killed in a riot by police and militia in 1849—the first time in US history that soldiers shot point blank into a crowd.[12]

It was clear on all sides that further convulsions were in the offing unless there was major social change. But it was workers who took the lead in trying to redirect the course of development:

> *While many different groups of New Yorkers began to advance their own so-*
> *lutions for an unrestrained individualism in the 1850s and 1860s, workers*
> *were at the fore. For no other group was imposing coherence on a new in-*
> *dustrial environment of rampant competition, topsy-turvy markets, persistent*
> *unemployment, and squalid living conditions... In a period of unprecedented*
> *organisational creativity, city workers devised scores of producer, consumer,*
> *and building co-operatives; presided over a citywide Industrial Congress in*
> *1850-51, an 'Amalgamated Trades Convention' in 1853, and a Working-*
> *men's Congress during the war; sent their own representatives to scores of*
> *'independent' reform meetings, and, finally, created the permanent trade*
> *unions celebrated by* [historian John R] *Commons. These new institutions*
> *were conceived at remove from the party oligarchies and were political in*
> *many instances. They were part of an effort to complement or replace an*
> *effete party system unresponsive to the problems of urban industrial life.*[13]

Yet the working class behind these struggles was anything but socially homogeneous. The industrial revolution was remaking the working class. The artisans who made up the core of New York's labouring population early in the century were, by the 1850s, being pulled in two directions. A minority were upwardly mobile, becoming masters who employed others. These mixed easily with the middle class and were the likeliest to participate in reform projects. Others faced downward social pressure. The spread of the factory system afforded fewer and fewer opportunities for apprentices to become journeymen, and journeymen to become masters. This layer of 'mechanics' was perhaps the largest section of the New York working class. The proletarianisation was furthest advanced among the degraded trades of textiles, shoemaking, and other labour intensive consumer goods industries. These were less likely to organise; their 'unions' were often industry associations which sometimes sent bosses to represent them at city wide meetings.[14]

The fastest growing section of the New York working class was the industrial worker. The mammoth Novelty Iron Works, which employed 1,000 workers, was typical of the new metal working industry in uptown Manhattan. Its employees were highly skilled and class conscious. Yet, like the more skilled artisans, these machinists were at the top of a workplace hierarchy. Machinists routinely employed subcontractors as assistants or finishers. Geographically removed from the mainstream of political life, they tended not to participate in trade union and political activity. Finally there was the mass of unskilled labourers, which by the late 1840s was almost exclusively composed of Irish immigrants and a small number of black workers.[15]

These divisions and subdivisions in this changing working class affected workers' trade union and political activity. While artisans and journeymen began to create their own organisations, unskilled labourers tended to give uncritical support to the Democratic Party machine. Politically the workers were united only by their hostility to the Republican Party.

Unlike the Democrats who sought to co-opt the incipient labour movement, the industrialists who pushed workplace paternalism and Protestant social reformism were hostile to organised labour. These employers were increasingly disturbed by the tendency of the local 'Democracy' to appease working class discontent with patronage and charity schemes. Democratic leaders like Mayor Fernando Wood saw workers less as class enemies than a loyal base of voters. The divisions in the ruling class over how to deal with the working class became an open split during the Depression of 1857. At an outdoor rally of unemployed workers Democratic Mayor Fernando Wood used radical language to lay the blame for the crisis at the feet of the industrialists:

Truly it may be said that in New York those who produce everything get nothing and those who produce nothing get everything. They labour without income whilst surrounded by thousands living in affluence and splendour, who have income without labour... Now, is it not our duty to provide some way to afford relief?[16]

Of course this speech did not go over well with the Republican merchants and industrialists. *New York Times* editor Henry Raymond excoriated Woods' 'communism' and compared him to the Parisian revolutionaries of 1848. Raymond's criticism anticipated the bread riots that erupted on 9 November when the city sponsored relief promised by Woods did not materialise.[17] Yet despite the riots, the Republican recriminations and Woods' subsequent political defeat, the Democrats did not alter their conciliatory approach to class struggle. The Democracy was controlled by merchants and financiers with close ties to the Southern slave economy, Western agriculture and trade with Europe. For the most part they did not share the immediate material interests or the consciousness of the Republican industrialists who aggressively sought to limit and shape workers' activity.[18] In fact, Democratic merchants sometimes bargained over the head of the stevedores directly with Irish longshoremen (dockers). In return they expected Irish workers to remember them on election day.[19] Thus, as the North-South sectional conflict sharpened in the 1850s, the New York Democracy steeped itself in populism—and white supremacy.[20]

The anti-draft riots

During the secession crisis between Lincoln's electoral victory in November 1860 and the Confederate attack on Fort Sumter, South Carolina, in April 1861, New York's Democratic merchants seriously considered secession for the city. Merchant August Belmont, soon to become the national chairman of the Democratic Party, wrote in a letter to a Southern businessman that, in the event of the breakup of the Union, 'New-York, in such a catastrophe, would cut loose from the Puritanical East and her protective tariff, and without linking her fortunes with our kind but somewhat exacting Southern friends, she would open her magnificent port to the commerce of the world'.[21]

But with the outbreak of the war the pro-Confederate rhetoric of the Democrats disappeared in an outburst of patriotic, pro-Union sentiment. Thousands of workers heeded the call of their Republican bosses to enlist. But by the fall of 1862 the Democrats had divided into pro-Lincoln 'War Democrat' and pro-Confederate 'Peace Democrat' factions. By 1863 the costs of the war were hitting Northern workers hard through massive inflation. Hostility to the intrusive, centralising Republican regime began to grow. In several parts of the North even pro-Union workers who struck for higher wages to keep pace with inflation found themselves forced back to work at gunpoint by the Union Army. State legislatures in Minnesota and Illinois outlawed strikes altogether. The Republican alliance of the 'producing classes' was under considerable stress.[22]

Moreover, a series of Northern military debacles had left the fate of the war hanging in the balance. The Emancipation Proclamation that went into effect on 1 January 1863 was seen by Lincoln as a necessary tactic to win the war, not a general turn to abolitionism. It applied only to slaves in Confederate territory, not to those in pro-Union slave states or Confederate areas occupied by the North. But its immediate effect was to accelerate the desertion of slaves from the South—what DuBois called the 'General Strike'.[23] By emancipating themselves the slaves crippled the Southern economy.

Nevertheless, the military stalemate forced Lincoln to institute a draft on 24 March 1863.[24] The draft was nakedly inequitable. It allowed a draftee to purchase his way out for $300—a considerable sum for the middle classes, to say nothing of workers. James McPherson argues that the inequity of the draft should not be overstated. Draft substitution for military service had been used in the revolution. Moreover, the $300 commutation fee was actually designed as a cap on the rising cost of procuring a substitute—'a way of bringing exemption within reach of the working class instead of discriminating against them… It was not conscription at all, but a clumsy carrot and stick device to stimulate volunteering. The stick was the threat of being drafted and the carrot was a bounty for volunteering.'[25]

The draft was bound to be controversial in New York City. Despite the election of a Republican mayor the city was still a Democratic stronghold.[26] On the morning of 13 July 1863 workers walked off their jobs to forcibly shut down the draft lottery. But by nightfall the riot had degenerated into an anti-black pogrom. When the riot ended five days later, 105 people were dead.[27] But not all workers responded to the draft by attacking blacks. The initial leaders of the anti-draft protest tended to be artisans or skilled workers such as fire fighters. Despite their hostility to the Republican Party, by then the party of black emancipation, these skilled workers largely avoided racist violence. Some even co-operated with authorities to restore order. The most politically conscious workers, the German Americans, also worked to stop the anti-black violence.[28]

The main perpetrators of the anti-black violence were unskilled Irish Catholic labourers who worked on the docks.

> By midweek [of the riot], the rioters had virtually emptied the waterfront of people of colour. The most violent racial purges of the tenement districts were the special province of the men and boys of labourer families. Black sailor William Williams was assaulted...when he walked ashore at an Upper West Side pier to ask directions. Like many of the racial murders, this attack developed into an impromptu neighbourhood theatre with its own horrific routines. Each member of the white gang came up to the prostrate sailor to perform an atrocity—to jump on him, smash his body with a cobblestone, plant a knife in his chest—while the white audience of local proprietors, workmen, women and boys watched the tragedy with a mixture of shock, fascination and, in most instances, a measure of approval.[29]

This violent anti-black behaviour by Irish immigrants was a relatively new phenomenon. As late as 1829 in Boston the Irish themselves were the targets of a race riot along with blacks, and in the 1830s the Irish did not much participate in the anti-abolitionist riots of the period.[30] But by the 1840s the increasingly desperate economic straits of the Irish, exacerbated by immigrants fleeing the famine, made Irish workers' leaders increasingly prone towards violence to keep the docks and other unskilled labouring positions 'Irish only'. This ban was directed not only against blacks, but German Americans as well.[31]

The Irish labourers' precarious economic condition and poverty made them ripe for the Democrats' programme of paternalism and white supremacy. Encouraged by the Democratic politicians, they saw poor free black workers as economic competitors and sought to literally eradicate them from the city. But the Irish immigrants' embrace of racist ideas was not simply an ideological reflection of a struggle for economic survival. It was cultivated and reinforced by the employers through the pro-slavery Democratic Party and the Catholic Church.

In these circumstances it was tragic but predictable that Irish workers would protest the class bias of the 1863 draft with unspeakably violent attacks on blacks. But, as Bernstein makes clear, the riots were also the beginning of an unprecedented confrontation between labour and capital, in which workers increasingly identified their employers with the forces of the state. For example, the New York Metropolitan Police had been created by the Republican Party during its city administration in the late 1850s. Lincoln's appointment of police chief John A Kennedy as provost marshall for the draft virtually turned the police into an arm of the White House. The rioters were highly conscious of this fact. Prominent abolitionists like *New York Tribune* editor Horace Greeley and other well known Republicans like the *New York Times* editor were also targeted by the Irish rioters.[32]

The industrial bosses found their shops closed by picketing rioters. And, if the iron workers did not for the most part join the anti-black pogrom, they did take the opportunity to challenge their employers by walking off the job:

> *The industrialists' patriotic appeals no doubt helped them to secure the loyalty of the employees who marched in anti-riot factory brigades in July 1863. But by early 1863 many iron workers had come to associate the Republican Party with both the hardships of the war and the oppressive behaviour of the employers who were trying to undermine the value of their labour with cheap immigrant and black 'contrabands'. The economy and politics of wartime distanced industrialists from the mass of workers who came to see their employers' shop-floor regime and the Republican national regime as related threats. The draft riots were the bloody culmination of the industrialists' long-term difficulties with the metropolitan working class.[33]*

For a week rioters fought pitched battles with police and federal troops, forced the closure of large factories and workshops, attacked the homes of the wealthy and looted the retail stores of the rising middle class. The organisation and duration of the conflict gave the riot an insurrectionary flavour, especially as Union troops moved into the city to suppress the revolt. Historian David Montgomery detects a 'desperate, revolutionary quality emerging among the rioters, many of whom exhibited a fierce heroism in defending their barricades... In the dying embers of a race riot were grotesque reflections of Paris's Bloody June Days.'[34]

The riots were a grave threat to the Union cause. The city's minority Radical Republicans demanded that Lincoln declare martial law, arguing that instability in New York could cost the war. Lincoln refused, instead appointing a loyal War Democrat to oversee federal troops in the city.

Lincoln wanted to work with local authorities rather than replace them. The President believed, probably rightly, that martial law in New York would only guarantee further unrest and aid the fortunes of the 'Peace Democrats' who were challenging him in the 1864 election. And so Lincoln tried to cobble together a political alliance across party lines that would pre-empt further upheavals. The President pressured local Republicans to allow War Democrats in the city council to make an unprecedented expenditure to pay for draft dispensation for any worker who wanted it. Other employers made 'draft insurance' schemes available through the workplace. The only consolation for the Radical Republicans was the raising of the all black New York 69th Regiment, which was awarded its colours by wealthy white Republican women at a rally of 100,000 in the spring of 1864. At the same time, wealthy Republicans donated $40,000—an enormous sum—to 2,500 black victims of the anti-draft riots. According to Bernstein, the pro-Union blacks became the model of the Republican philanthropists' 'deserving poor'. In the absence of any stable mediating structures between capital and labour, a divided ruling class used different strategies to achieve class peace. The Democratic merchants took patronage to its logical conclusions, using public funds to purchase dispensation for the draft. The Republicans, frustrated in their bid to crush working class rebelliousness through martial law, sought to shape the lives of free blacks through paternalism.[35]

From draft riots to the eight hour movement

The racism of larger numbers of white workers became tragically clear in anti-draft riots in New York City in 1863. But the potential for working class struggle that could overcome those divisions was also in evidence. The class peace established through the draft insurance evaporated before the end of the civil war. The 1864 elections already saw New York workers running candidates on the platform of the eight hour day. By 1868 workers' demands got through the ascendancy of the Radical Republicans. The Radicals' version of Reconstruction brought blacks into Southern state governments and Congress, and raised the possibility of the large scale expropriation and redistribution of the slaveholders' land. This explicit challenge to property gave impetus to the eight hour movement in the North, and opened the door for an alliance of Southern freed black slaves and Northern white workers.[36]

Moreover, the war had deeply politicised tens of thousands of worker soldiers. The Union Army was a place where a white worker might hear lectures on Marxism from a German officer. Potentially just as radicalising was the experience of meeting and fighting alongside black soldiers, who came to number 180,000. Although Irish immigrants made up a relatively small minority of the Union Army, a significant number found the army to be a path out of the ghetto and the Democratic Party. Fenianism, revolutionary Irish nationalism, flourished in the Union Army. And, crucially for the unity of the postbellum labour movement, Protestant workers' experience fighting alongside Irish and German workers helped break down their anti-immigrant nativism.[37]

Workers' expectations rose with the end of the war, leading to the formation in 1866 of the National Labor Union (NLU), the first genuinely national trade union organisation in the US. Prominent trade union leader William Sylvis wrote in an early NLU circular:

> *The working-people of our nation, white and black, male and female, are sinking to a condition of serfdom. Even now a slavery exists in our land worse than ever existed under the old slave system. The centre of the slave-power no longer exists south of Mason's and Dixon's line. It has been transferred to Wall Street... This movement we are now engaged in is the great anti-slavery movement, and we must push on the work of emancipation until slavery is abolished in every corner of our country... Then will come such a social revolution as the world has never witnessed; honest industry in every department will receive its just reward, and public thieves will be compelled to make an honest living or starve. **Let us all go to work.**[38]*

Sylvis's statement obviously reflects racism. He was of course wrong to say that workers' conditions were 'worse' than that of slaves. Moreover, he criticised the mingling of blacks and whites under Reconstruction. Although he was for an independent labour party, Sylvis favoured the white supremacist Democrats in the 1868 elections on the grounds that the Republicans were dominated by Wall Street.[39] But unlike the antebellum labour movement, when Democratic influenced leaders used the term 'wage-slavery' to disparage the abolitionism, the NLU was attempting to emphasise the *continuity* between black emancipation, abolitionism and postbellum labour reform.

The NLU did not organise blacks, even after blacks were used as strike breakers in the postbellum strikes of 1866. Some trade unionists and labour advocates bitterly criticised the NLU for this stance. One NLU leader addressed the convention's second convention in 1867 on the question of the status of the freed slaves:

> *They number four million strong, and a greater proportion of them labour with their hands than can be counted from among the same number of any other people on earth. Their moral influence, and their strength at the ballot-box, would be of incalculable value to the cause of labour. Can we afford to reject their proferred co-operation and make them enemies? By committing*

*such an act of folly we would inflict greater injury upon the cause of Labour
Reform than the combined efforts of capital could accomplish...*[40]

The appeal fell on deaf ears. Only one union, the Boston carpenters'
and joiners' union, admitted blacks. More typical was the experience of
Frederick Douglass's son, who was barred from the Washington DC
typesetters' union because he was black. The persistence of racism did
force black workers to organise separately in the Colored National Labor
Union.[41]

The NLU's unwillingness to organise blacks highlighted what Eric
Foner called 'the inescapable reality that white labour did not wish to cooperate with black'.[42] Robert Allen rightly observed that 'racial prejudice
and fear of economic competition virtually nullified the NLU's official
policy of racial co-operation'.[43] But the NLU's shortcomings must be
seen not in isolation, but as part of the uneven first steps in the development of an anti-racist current in the organised labour movement. It
would be idealism to expect the social and ideological transformations of
the civil war, profound though they were, to immediately and completely
transform white workers' consciousness with regard to blacks. It is important to note that the formative years of the NLU came before the
onset of Radical Reconstruction and the largest strikes for the eight hour
day. The NLU's steps towards links with black workers, however
limited, were nonetheless significant. Black delegates attended the 1869
convention of the NLU, which formally adopted a policy of co-operation
with black workers. This was largely untested as the NLU declined in
the early 1870s. But the 1869 convention did demonstrate a small but
growing tendency towards inter-racial labour solidarity.

The situation was complicated politically when the struggle for the
eight hour day divided the Radical Republicans. The Republican ideology of 'free soil, free labour, free men' was elastic enough for a broad
class alliance of Northern industrialists, farmers and workers to defeat
the slave power. But to Republican industrialists, 'free labour' was the
freedom of market forces and the possibility of individual upward mobility—not the freedom of workers to organise. By 1870 this ideology
no longer fitted the objective circumstances. Of the 12.9 million people
in all occupations, 4.9 million were non-agricultural wage earners and
3.7 million were agricultural wage earners. David Montgomery sums up
the contradiction at the heart of Republican ideology:

*The fact that two out of three productively engaged Americans were hirelings
posed an ideological dilemma for the free-labour system. Americans associated liberty with the ownership of private property. Its opposite—lack of
property—was thus a form of slavery, and in fact the phrase 'wage slavery'*

enjoyed widespread and respectable use at mid-century. But what a paradox for the 'free-labour system' to generate wage slavery! [44]

The growing splits in the Republican Party created an opening for socialists, particularly in the labour movement centre of New York. The Republicans' base among industrialists and their hardline response to the draft riots had already put them, as far as organised labour was concerned, in the enemy camp. Indeed, while Radical Republicans in other parts of the country were trying to extend popular democracy, the New York Radicals sought to limit it through 'reform' of state laws. And, as Bernstein shows, the Democratic merchants and financiers had already strained their relationship with labour by moving towards an accommodation with Northern industrialists.

The postbellum crisis and flux in the two 'regular' parties coincided with the establishment of New York sections of the International Workingmen's Association (IWA, the First International) led by Karl Marx's close comrade, Fredreich Sorge. Starting from a base among the city's German speaking workers, the IWA was involved in the (temporarily successful) struggles of New York's powerful building trades workers for an eight hour day.[45] One of the sections of the New York IWA affiliated to the NLU as Labor Union No 5, and in 1869 quickly set about organising a black union. The IWA not only provided a meeting hall for black workers, but successfully fought for the admission of black workers in the Workingmen's Union, the central labour body in New York. The IWA was bitterly split between Marxists and anti-Marxist factions who tailed middle class reformism.[46] Nevertheless, the intervention of these socialists underscored the possibilities of inter-racial labour organising in the United States—even in New York City, the home of the 1863 race riot.

The National Labor Union and the Colored National Labor Union organised separately. But the growth of the postbellum economy soon drew black and white workers into the same workplaces, particularly on the railroads. After a downturn in struggle following the depression of 1873, the Great Labour Uprising of 1877 was conclusive evidence that a national labour movement had arrived. The strike wave also made it clear that black and white workers had a common interest in, and capacity for, united organisation against capital. J P McDonnell, the Marxist editor of the newspaper *Labor Standard*, pointed this in New York City at a workers' mass meeting in solidarity with the strikers:

It was a grand sight to see in West Virginia, white and coloured men standing together, men of all nationalities in one supreme contest for the common rights of Workingmen. (Loud cheers). The barriers of ignorance and prejudice were fast falling before the growing intelligence of the masses. Here-

after there shall be no north, no south, no east, no west, only one land of
labour and the workingmen must own and possess it.[47]

The unity McDonnell saw proved to be fragile. In St Louis the strike
centre threatened to split along racial lines as the strike headed for defeat
and in San Francisco workers attacked Chinese immigrants. Yet what is
crucial is that the first national strike in the US could never have happened if the initial organising committees had not included both black
and white workers.[48]

The increasing tempo of class struggle led even many Radical Republicans to turn their backs on labour. The administration of Republican President Grant became increasingly conscious of a need to defend
private property from popular challenge in the North as well as the
South. It began to withdraw political support for the redistribution of
land that was to have been at the heart of Radical Reconstruction. The
result was, in Eric Foner's words, an 'unfinished revolution'.[49]

Black workers in New York

There is one serious weakness in Bernstein's book: the failure to devote
sufficient attention to New York's black workers. There is no question of
Bernstein's sympathies for the victims of these pogroms. He does not
shy away from or apologise for the horrors of white supremacy and its
crippling effect on the labour movement. Indeed, he obliquely criticises
Marx's failure to stress to his American comrades the necessity to build
links between black and white workers as well as between German and
Irish immigrants.[50] But Bernstein presents blacks not as self active and
politically conscious subjects, but as objects. Blacks appear as the targets
of the Irish unskilled labourers' fear and loathing, and the Peace
Democrats' pro-Confederate demagoguery, the model 'deserving poor'
of the Union Club capitalists' philanthropy, and, as the all black New
York 69th Regiment, the tool of a Republican administration compelled
to use revolutionary methods to end the war.

We know that black workers in New York were pushed out of skilled
positions. In 1850, 75 percent of the black workers in New York were
employed in menial or unskilled positions. By 1857 that figure reached
87.5 percent.[51] Bernstein's evident research skills could have certainly
been used to tell us more about the black workers' response to the riot.
How many sought refuge outside New York? How many returned during
or after the war, and when? How many joined the 69th Regiment? Who
among them participated in New York City's eight hour movements—
perhaps alongside ex-rioters?

These are not only questions of racial balance in historiography, but
are absolutely crucial in meeting the tasks Bernstein sets for himself: to

explain the dynamics of race and class in New York City, and by implication the US, at mid-century. A full assessment must provide more information about black workers than Bernstein provides.

The 'unfinished revolution' and working class racism

Bernstein's account of the years from the anti-black pogrom of 1863 to
the eight hour day movement of the late 1860s is one of the most dramatic examples of white workers' racist ideas breaking down in struggle.
Under the revolutionary impact of the civil war, white workers rejected
the Democrats and white supremacy and took major strides towards
inter-racial trade union unity and independent politics in the postbellum
era. Yet for many on the US left, such changes in white workers' consciousness are seen as anomalous—if they are acknowledged at all. Even
Eric Foner, a Marxist and the leading historian of Reconstruction as an
'unfinished revolution', writes: 'The continued existence of second class
status for free blacks more than a century after the abolition of slavery
changes the *terms* but not the *essence* of this contradiction between
racism and equality, which lies in the slavery period' [emphasis added].[52]

Similarly, in an essay on 'The Demand for Black Labour' Harold
Baron contends that 'abolition of slavery did not mean substantive
freedom to the black worker. He was basically confined to racially
defined agrarian labour in which he was more exploited than any class of
whites, even the landless poor.'[53]

The persistence of racism has led others to conclude that whites
benefit from (mainly anti-black) racism and that therefore race is at least
as fundamental a social division as class. Former labour and civil rights
lawyer Herbert Hill is perhaps extreme, but certainly not alone in asserting that trade unions are the actual agency of black oppression in the
US.[54] It follows from such views that Marxism's alleged 'class reduc-
tionism' is inadequate for, if not a hindrance to, an understanding of race
and class in the United States. Therefore, the argument goes, the Marxist
strategy of building a revolutionary socialist party—to say nothing of
workers' power—on an inter-racial basis is flawed, if not utopian.[55]
More than a few Marxists accept such claims or make concessions to
them. A recent example is American labour historian David R Roediger's analysis of white workers' attitudes towards blacks in the period
1800-65. Generically criticising Marxists for 'privileging' class over
race, Roediger builds on WEB DuBois' view of white supremacy as a
'public and psychological wage' to compensate for their own exploitation. Roediger implies that the antebellum era was the decisive 'formative period of working class "whiteness".'[56]

Yet it is precisely the years *after* 1865 which showed that white workers could rethink and break from the anti-black racism that appeared to be so deeply rooted in the antebellum period. Because he generalises wrongly from the pre-1865 period, Roediger's view of the potential of whites to break with racism is distorted—and inevitably pessimistic. As Paul D'Amato points out, such an argument 'blurs the difference between a workers' *perception* of benefiting from racism and the reality: that their conditions are degraded and held down by racism'.[57]

Nevertheless, Roediger is forced to acknowledge that white racism is 'shaped behind the dams of repression' and can be 'swept away dramatically when the dams begin to break'.[58] The implication is clear: working class 'whiteness' was an *ideological* construct of discipline minded antebellum bosses and pro-slavery politicians, developed in a relatively short period. But the ideology of white supremacy was profoundly challenged in the revolutionary context of the emancipation of 4 million black slaves, the destruction of the slaveholders as a class and the radical democracy of Reconstruction. The eight hour movement of the late 1860s and the early 1870s and the Great Labour Uprising of 1877 were indeed the 'burst dams' that opened the way for inter-racial labour solidarity.

The Great Labour Uprising of 1877 went down to defeat, and the labour organisations of that period dissolved. But, however short lived, inter-racial labour unity had been achieved on a scale unimaginable—and, as Marx argued, impossible—as long as blacks were enslaved. Indeed, the spectre of inter-racial working class rebellion was a key factor in the reactionary Compromise of 1877, in which the Republicans held on to the presidency with a minority of the votes in exchange for the withdrawal of US troops from the South and restoration of Democratic political control there.[59]

The end of Reconstruction in the South brought new 'Redeemer Democrat' state governments, which set about institutionalising white supremacy. The pressure of white racism on the labour movement increased. Yet the main labour organisation of the 1880s, the Knights of Labor, continued to organise blacks as well as whites. Although the Knights kept no records of black or white membership, one leader estimated that in 1886 of 700,000 members 60,000 were black. A year later a New York newspaper put the figure at 90,000 to 95,000.[60]

This substantial black membership is more impressive when it is recalled that the Knights were really a hybrid of trade union and political party, organised by region rather than workplace and deeply involved in workers' lives outside the workplace.[61] They stood out as virtually the only integrated institution in the South.[62] This provided a new dimension for black and white workers' solidarity. As one historian puts it:

Though keenly aware of racial hostility in the South and of the basically anti-union sentiment in that region, the Knights attempted to organise black and white workers in all areas of the South. Most revolutionary of all, the national leaders insisted that race was of no consequence in economic questions facing workers.[63]

The Knights' record of anti-racism was not perfect. Some Southern assemblies remained segregated, either because of public pressure or the racism of white members. And, as the Knights declined in the mid-1880s and drifted towards accommodation with the Democratic Party, sections of the California Knights were involved in the virulent anti-Chinese campaign.[64] Nevertheless, the Knights' resistance to the dominant trend towards white supremacy is nothing less than remarkable. It was only through the most severe repression that the Knights were defeated in the South. A typical example was in 1887, when a strike of 6,000 to 10,000 black workers was defeated only when planters used arms—including a Gatling machine gun—to kill dozens of strikers.[65]

By 1885-6 the nationwide struggle for the eight hour day was back. The Knights were quickly bypassed, because of both their geographic organisation and their political adaptation to the Democrats. A new leadership of anarchists and socialists had emerged in what would become the American Federation of Labor (AFL). The anti-racist radical political current created by the civil war had not only survived reaction, but was strengthening.[66]

A red scare and a wave of anti-labour repression followed the Chicago Haymarket police riot of 1886. But even the conspiracy trial and execution of Albert Parsons and three others did not destroy the revolutionary tendencies. By the early 1890s another wave of working class militancy had erupted—this time in a loose alliance with the radical— and inter-racial—Populist farmers' movement. The defeat of this movement, epitomised by the workers' loss in the great rail strike of 1894, came on the heels of a major defeat for inter-racial unionism in the South. Rural Populism was also smashed. Mike Davis summarised the implications of the defeat:

First, the united rebellion of the Southern yeomen and farm tenants—the cutting edge of Agrarian radicalism—was broken up by a violent counter-attack of the regional ruling class which counterposed 'Jim Crow' [segregation] and redneck demagogism to the Farmers' Alliance and inter-racial co-operation. A vicious panoply of black disfranchisement, racial segregation, and lynch terror was installed in the 1890s to suppress militant black tenants, to keep them tied to the land, and to prevent their future collaboration with poor whites. At the same time, the defeat of the Great New Orleans General Strike of 1892 destroyed the vanguard of Southern labour and wrecked inter-racial unity among workers. Out of its ashes arose a stunted, Jim Crow white unionism on one hand, and a pariah black sub-proletariat on the other... Secondly, this Southern counter-revolution was paralleled north of the Mason-Dixon Line by a resurgence of nativism and ethno-religious conflict within the Northern industrial working class... Fatally for the hopes of labour radicals, anti-immigrant and anti-Catholic prejudice rent the unity of even those industrial unions, the miners and the railway workers, which were ostensibly the bedrock of Labour-Populism...[67]

It was these staggering defeats, not the inherent racism of white workers, that led to the consolidation of segregation in the South. The fact that the heyday of white supremacy came fully three decades after the civil war is evidence of the strong impulse towards inter-racial solidarity in the workers' movement and even among farmers. The trade union defeats of the early 1890s and the incorporation of Populism into the Democratic Party commenced a long downturn in class struggle. The AFL leadership abandoned socialism and moved towards craftism, colour bars and the Democratic Party. In this reactionary climate the new American Socialist Party was soon dominated by its middle class racist right wing rather than its anti-racist militant left. The labour movement of the 1890s confronted a nearly unbroken string of Republican administrations and systematic union busting from the Republican captains of industry. This enabled the Democrats in the labour strongholds in north eastern cities to compete with the Socialists for the role of opposition to big business. (This was despite the fact that the Southern Democrats— the Dixiecrats—were viciously anti-labour. The largely agricultural Southern economy did not interest the rightward moving labour leaders.) The trade union bureaucrats thus adapted to white supremacy, using it to justify and maintain a labour movement based on the narrow confines of craft. By stressing control of the market of skilled labour, craft unionism excluded not only unskilled blacks but most Southern and Eastern European immigrants.[68]

In the South the downfall of Reconstruction meant that blacks were not only denied the 40 acres and a mule promised to them by the radicals, but were, in WEB DuBois' words, pushed 'backward toward slavery'.[69] Yet being pushed back towards slavery is not the same as being enslaved. The revolutionary impact of black emancipation was blunted but not overturned. Certainly the apartheid-like political strictures on blacks reinforced white supremacy and severely limited the scope for black and white workplace unity. But despite the denial of *political* rights for Southern blacks, the civil war had wrought fundamental *social* change. Market forces were inexorably drawing black and white labour together to confront a common enemy: the employer. That is why Eric Foner is completely wrong to claim that 'the abolition of slavery changes the *terms* but not the *essence* of [the] contradiction between racism and equality'. The overthrow of slavery meant that the United States would not develop South African style full blown apartheid, in which black workers would be restricted to a separate labour market and an embourgeoisified white working class would develop material interests binding them to the state.[70] Instead black and white workers' common condition as free wage labourers created objective common interests—not only in 'equality', but in socialism and black liberation.

Thus Harold Baron, after asserting that blacks did not win 'substantive freedom' with abolition, is forced to acknowledge that:

Abrogation of the slave system had made possible some new types of mobility among both blacks and whites, bringing about changes in the forms of inter-racial conflict and class conflict. Blacks were now able to move geographically, even in the face of continued legal and extralegal restraints. The migration that took place was mainly a westerly one within the South. Inside the black community, class mobility developed through the emergence of a small middle class.[71]

Compared to slavery, this was indeed 'substantive freedom'. Blacks were largely excluded from the new Southern textile industry, and many were jailed on trumped up charges in order to be leased out as convict labourers. But there was, nevertheless, a 'rather considerable increase in industrial employment of blacks between 1890 and 1910...in railroading, lumbering, and coal mining—that is, in non-factory type operations with these three industries often located in rural areas'.[72] Crucially, in these industries, the ex-slaves and their descendants worked alongside whites. Thus some of the most important examples of white and black workers' solidarity in the late 19th century came not in the North, but in the heartland of white supremacy. Against all the odds—and violent repression—the Industrial Workers of the World organised black and white lumber workers in the South.[73] In the coalfields of Alabama the tradition of inter-racial organising began with the Great Labour Uprising of 1877 and dramatically re-emerged in violent strikes in 1894, 1904 and 1908, at the height of the racist Jim Crow terror and colour bars in the Northern craft unions.[74]

It took the boom created by the First World War to pull black workers into the North. The wartime labour shortage was exacerbated by the drying up of European immigration, and blacks moved into the new mass production industries of steel and meat packing. The post-war strikes in those industries were the peak of the greatest strike wave in US history up to that point. It also saw the disastrous impact of segregation on US labour. The 'Red Summer' of 1919 got its name not because of the considerable influence of socialists in the strikes, but because of the bloody race riots in Chicago and other Northern cities. The employers systematically used black workers as strikebreakers, often without informing them that they were taking other workers' jobs. Many blacks crossed picket lines because the unions would not admit them as members.[75]

Racism destroyed the 1919 strike wave. This defeat, along with the split of the Socialist Party over the Russian Revolution, had enormous consequences. The left wing of the Socialist Party and the Industrial Workers of the World had been real contenders for the leadership of the labour movement. But the near total collapse of industrial unionism after 1919 strengthened the craftist AFL labour bureaucrats and their alliance with the Democrats. This time the alliance was institutionalised under the auspices of Democratic President Wilson's War Labor Board. The weakness of the left in the post-war open shop drive led to what one historian calls 'the fall of the house of labour'.[76] 'It would be difficult to exaggerate the magnitude of American labour's defeat in the 1919-24 period. For almost a decade the corporations were virtually free from the challenge of militant unionism.'[77]

White workers' racism both contributed to and was reinforced by this defeat. But the growth of mass production industry that employed blacks as well as whites created the objective basis for inter-racial unity. The crisis of the Great Depression provided a tremendous opening for the anti-racist labour left. By the late 1930s a wave of strikes led to the creation of the Congress of Industrial Organizations (CIO), organised on an inter-racial basis.[78] The rise of the CIO also revived the tendency towards independent labour politics. But the pro-Democratic Party class collaborationism of the labour bureaucracy—supported by the Communist Party in its popular front phase—once again undercut labour's potential for a political break with the Democrats.[79] Nevertheless, the inter-racial character of the labour movement was fully established, even in the South. In 1930s Alabama the Communist Party could make dramatic breakthroughs in inter-racial industrial unionism.[80] The racist hate strikes of the Second World War were an exception in a general trend towards stable inter-racial trade union organisations.[81]

'Stability', of course, meant bureaucratisation. AFL-CIO leaders generally preferred the status quo alliance with the Democratic Party and opposed the insurgent black workers in the Civil Rights and Black Power movements of the 1960s. Most union leaders opposed affirmative action. But the vicious 'white backlash' orchestrated by the ruling class in the late 1960s did not include anti-black violence in the workplace, as had occurred so many times before in US history. Rather, an increasing number of white workers were prepared to follow black workers' lead in trade union struggles.[82]

None of this is to argue that inter-racial labour unity flows 'automatically' from workplace struggles over economic issues, or that successful trade union struggles lead directly to white workers' consciousness of, and commitment to overthrowing, black oppression. The eruption of racist hate strikes during the Second World War made that clear. The point is that the objective unity of black and white workers at the workplace creates the potential for these shifts in white workers' consciousness. Whether or not such potential has been realised in the US labour movement has depended in large part on the intervention of labour militants, particularly socialists, to build a unity principled and strong enough to survive the bosses' inevitable divide and rule tactics and the trade union bureaucracy's equally inevitable accommodation to racism.

In 'normal' times most white workers are racist. But the dominant ideas in any society are the ideas of the ruling class. In 19th century America the ruling ideas —the ideology of white supremacy—were promulgated among white workers first through the agency of the antebellum Democratic Party, then by the emerging labour bureaucracy which came to serve as a conduit for the postbellum Democrats' ideas. It is sheer idealism to believe that white workers will break with racism on a *mass* scale except in periods of social and political upheaval. The civil war and Reconstruction, were, of course, exactly that. The eventual triumph of reaction should not obscure the reality of the revolutionary character of the civil war and its enduring impact on the US labour movement.

Through its analysis of the modern labour movement's origins in the revolutionary context of the civil war, Iver Bernstein's *The New York City Draft Riots* demonstrates how US workers, in the process of becoming a class for themselves, moved away from white supremacy and the Democratic Party towards a vision of a genuinely inter-racial workers' movement. The persistence of that tendency in the face of incredible defeats points directly to the possibility of socialism and black liberation in the United States.

Finally, Bernstein's book helps us understand the contradiction at the core of the Democratic Party: the incorporation of the labour movement into an openly capitalist political party. That contradiction is bound to re-emerge in the current period of economic and political crisis. Socialists will once again have the chance to provide an alternative.

Notes
1 Quoted in WEB DuBois, *Black Reconstruction in America, 1860-1880* (New York, 1985), p61
2 A Callinicos, 'Bourgeois Revolutions and Historical Materialism', in *International Socialism*, 43 (London, 1989), p151
3 K Marx and F Engels, *The Civil War in the United States*, (New York, 1974), p81
4 K Marx, *Capital* Vol I (New York, 1967), p301

5   DR Roediger, *The Wages of Whiteness: Race and the Making of the America Working Class*' (London, 1991), p14

6   A Shawki, 'Black Liberation and Socialism in the United States' in *International Socialism*, 47 (London, 1990), pp18-19

7   Quoted in H Aptheker, *Abolitionism: A Revolutionary Movement* (Boston, 1989), p 44

8   Ibid, p48.

9   E Magdol, *The Anti-Slavery Rank and File* (New York, 1986) quoted in ibid, p46.

10 E Foner, 'Workers and Slavery', in P Buhle and A Dawley (eds), *Working for Democracy: American Workers from the Revolution to the Present* (Urbana, Illinois, 1985), p23.

11 S Willentz, *Chants Democratic: New York City and the Rise of the American Working Class, 1788-1850* (New York, 1984), pp363-389.

12 I Bernstein, *The New York City Draft Riots* p149.

13 Ibid, p77.

14 Ibid, pp78-104.

15 Ibid, pp108-124.

16 Ibid, p138.

17 Ibid, p140.

18 Ibid, pp133-135.

19 Ibid, p118.

20 DR Roediger, op cit, p141.

21 I Bernstein, op cit, p144.

22 B Mandel, *Labor: Free and Slave, Workingmen and the Anti-Slavery Movement in the United States* (New York, 1955), p183; D Montgomery, *Beyond Equality: Labor and the Radical Republicans, 1862-1872* (Urbana, Illinois, 1980), pp97-101.

23 WEB DuBois, op cit, pp67-84.

24 JM McPherson, op cit, p600.

25 JM McPherson, op cit, pp603-605.

26 Bernstein, op cit, pp7-12.

27 Ibid, p5.

28 Ibid, pp17-42.

29 Ibid, p28.

30 DR Roediger, op cit, p134.

31 Ibid, p148.

32 I Bernstein, op cit, pp25, 37.

33 Ibid, pp186-187.

34 D Montgomery, op cit, p106.

35 I Bernstein, op cit, pp54-60.

36 D Montgomery, op cit, pp230-260.

37 Ibid, pp127-134.

38 B Mandel, op cit, p206.

39 PS Foner, *Organized Labor and the Black Worker, 1619-1981* (New York, 1981), p23.

40 Ibid, p21.

41 Ibid pp24-29.

42 E Foner, *Reconstruction*, p480.

43 R Allen, *Reluctant Reformers: Racism and Social Reform in the United States* (Washington DC, 1983), p189.

44 D Montgomery, op cit, p 30.

45 DR Roediger and PS Foner, *On Our Own Time: A History of American Labor and the Working Day* (New York, 1989), pp112-116.

46 PS Foner, *Organized Labor*, p27; D Montgomery, op cit, pp404-421.

47 PS Foner, *The Great Labor Uprising of 1877* (New York, 1977), p122.
48 DR Roediger, *Wages*, pp167-168.
49 E Foner, *Reconstruction*, pp553-601.
50 I Bernstein, op cit, p114.
51 H Baron, 'The Demand for Black Labor', in J Green (ed), *Workers' Struggles, Past and Present: a 'Radical America' Reader* (Philadelphia, 1983), p31.
52 E Foner, 'Workers and Slavery', in P Buhle and A Dawley (eds), op cit, p21.
53 H Baron, op cit, p34.
54 H Hill, 'Race, Ethnicity and Organized Labor: The Opposition to Affirmative Action', in *New Politics Vol I, No 2 (New Series)* (New York, 1987), pp31-82.
55 See CJ Robinson, *Black Marxism: The Making of the Black Radical Tradition* (London, 1983), pp2, 282-324.
56 DR Roediger, *Wages*, pp6-15.
57 P D'Amato, 'US Rulers Divided Both to Conquer Each', in *Socialist Worker* (Chicago, November 1991), p11.
58 DR Roediger, *Wages*, p176.
59 E Foner, *Reconstruction*, pp583-587.
60 PS Foner, *The History of Organized Labor in the United States*, (New York, 1980) Vol 2, pp66-67.
61 M Davis, *Prisoners of the American Dream* (London, 1986), pp30-33.
62 R Allen, op cit, p190.
63 WH Harris, *The Harder We Run: Black Workers Since the Civil War* (New York, 1982), p27.
64 EC Sandmeyer, *The Anti-Chinese Movement in California* (Urbana, Illinois, 1973), p98.
65 WH Harris, op cit, p28.
66 DR Roediger and P S Foner, *On Our Own Time*, pp123-144.
67 M Davis, op cit, pp38-39.
68 See D Montgomery, *The Fall of the House of Labor: The Workplace, the State and American Labor Activism, 1865-1925* (New York, 1989), pp257-330.
69 WEB DuBois, op cit, p708.
70 A Callinicos, *South Africa between Reform and Revolution* (London, 1988), pp10-16.
71 H Baron, op cit, pp35-36.
72 Ibid, p37.
73 M Dubofsky, *We Shall Be All: A History of the Industrial Workers of the World* (New York, 1969), pp213-220.
74 R L Lewis, *Black Coal Miners in America* (Lexington, Kentucky, 1987), pp40-57.
75 P S Foner, *Organized Labor*, pp144-146.
76 For an overview see D Montgomery, *Fall*, pp370-464.
77 M Davis, op cit, p51.
78 P S Foner, *Organized Labor*, pp215-237.
79 L Selfa, *Socialists and the Democratic Party: A Lesser Evil?* (Chicago, 1988), pp6, 25-26.
80 See RDG Kelly, *Hammer and Hoe: Alabama Communists During the Great Depression* (Chapel Hill, North Carolina, 1990).
81 M Glaberman, *Wartime Strikes* (Detroit, 1980), pp6-34.
90 See D Georgakas and M Surkin, *Detroit: I Do Mind Dying: A Study in Urban Revolution* (New York, 1975).

The prospects for socialists—
an interview with Tony Cliff

LINDSEY GERMAN AND PETER MORGAN

There are all sorts of reasons being put forward for Labour's recent defeat. Why do you think Labour lost the General Election?

The overwhelming reason why Labour lost was because the Labour Party campaign did not reflect the massive anger which exists against the Tories. Every time there has been any struggle, Labour has taken a lead in the opinion polls. For example, in April 1990, after the big demonstrations against the poll tax, Labour was 24.5 points ahead of the Tories. By the time of the election this lead had been dissipated. What happened to this anger? People are not better off than they were two years ago, and the Tories' policies are just as unpopular.

Two things happened over that time. Firstly, Thatcher, who was the focus for resentment, was replaced by Major. That took away a central symbol of the anger. In addition, the Labour leaders did their best not to tap into the anger that existed. During the election campaign the poll tax was hardly mentioned, and there was certainly no real campaign against it. Yet Labour could have tapped the huge numbers affected by the tax. There were 11 million poll tax summonses for non-payment, there were 1.25 million under warrant for non-payment in Scotland, and up to 1 million benefit deductions. The Local Government Information Unit estimates there were 15 to 17 million people who had not paid the tax for at least some period. If these people alone had voted Labour its total vote would have increased, and Labour would have had a majority of over 100.

On other issues, such as low pay, little was done. The minimum wage was very popular with ordinary people, but the Labour leadership was not aggressive over the issue. Instead they were very defensive. They should have made it an issue over which to attack the Tories, by comparing the low paid with those at the top like the bosses who have gained so much under the Tories. That would have struck a chord, but it was not done. Instead of this Labour leaders hardly ever raised the issue of the minimum wage; they only reacted to the Tory accusation that the minimum wage would increase unemployment.

Occasionally, some class content did appear in Labour's propaganda. Its high point was the health broadcast, Jennifer's ear, which caused such a storm. On this issue Labour could have massively increased its support, but the moment the Tories went on the offensive the Labour leadership backed down and the issue was lost. So there was little concentration on the emergence of a two tier system in the NHS. There was no campaign by Labour over the spread of poverty in this country. Housing was hardly mentioned. No one said that there were 200,000 council houses a year built during the 1950s, whereas there were only 13,000 council houses built last year. On every issue which galvanises real anger among people, Labour failed to fight. It therefore threw away the lead in the polls and ended up defeated, because it tried to play the Tories at their own game.

However, none of this alone explains the Labour Party defeat. For that we have to look much deeper. Labour's aim of managing capitalism more efficiently and humanely than the Tories has got them into this position. So, for example, one reason why the poll tax was downplayed was because Labour councils are committed to collecting it, to the extent of sending working class people to prison for non-payment. The whole approach is to convince British capitalism that Labour can run the system.

So the Labour leadership has spent the last few years appealing to the City of London—the 'prawn cocktail circuit'—which has meant attacking any struggle or policy which might upset the City. And of course the City of London showed its gratitude to John Smith and Neil Kinnock—when Labour lost, the value of shares rose by £20 billion, and in 24 hours the government sold as many bonds as it would usually sell in a month.

However, it would be a mistake to assume that Labour lost the election during the four weeks of the campaign, or even in the three months before. Much of the rot had set in long before. Throughout the 1980s, when the Labour leadership argued for new realism, when they told workers to wait for a Labour victory, they were making it much more likely that they would lose the next election. Without collective action, workers' confidence declined. Yet over the last years Kinnock has argued to dampen the action among one group of workers after another. This is the main reason for their defeat. Again and again during the long years of Tory rule the outbreak of class conflicts pushed Labour support forward—in 1980 during the steel strike Labour had 8 percent advantage over the Tories; in 1981 during the inner city riots Labour had 10 percent advantage; in 1984/85 during the miners' strike this was 14 to 15 percent; in 1990 during the ambulance dispute it was 16 percent; and following the poll tax mass demonstrations and riots of March 1990 Labour's advantage was 24.5 percent. In the name of new realism, however, the Labour leaders dampened workers' struggles and this parliamentary cretinism led to the failure of Labour in the parliamentary elections of 1992.

None of this was inevitable. In this election left wing candidates often made a very good showing—usually because they campaigned on some sort of class politics. For example in Coventry South-East the expelled Labour MP Dave Nellist (who stood as Independent Labour) nearly won, but more importantly the left majority increased massively if you add the official and unofficial Labour vote. The same happened in Liverpool Broad Green. Bernie Grant in Tottenham tripled his majority.

Why does Labour as a whole not do this, and why has it moved so far to the right in recent years?

In order to understand it, we need to look at the history of British capitalism since the war. From 1945 to 1974 there was the post-war consensus between the two main parties, based on very similar policies.

This period of consensus was sometimes termed 'Butskellism' and was based on certain shared assumptions. Full employment was accepted by both Labour and the Tories. So for example in the early 1970s when unemployment reached 1 million under the Heath government there was a massive outcry. There were a couple of hundred factory occupations and Heath was forced to do a U-turn and cut unemployment. It was cut to 600,000. The second agreement was the mixed economy—that there had to be a balance between the state and private sectors. Thirdly, there was a commitment to the welfare state. So Harold Macmillan, the Minister of Housing in the Churchill government, boasted that he was the best one ever because he built over 200,000 houses in one year. Both parties were committed to building council houses.

However, although it was always true that there was consensus, the parties' policies were not identical. The Tories did not mind a little unemployment when there was 'full employment', and saw it as preferable to an inflationary economy. This was much less acceptable to Labour. Labour put more emphasis on the public sector while the Tories emphasised the private sector, and the Labour Party was also more committed to the welfare state. But neither talked about any fundamental change in the set up. The expansion of British capitalism between 1945 and the early 1970s was such that these reforms could be achieved.

From 1974 onwards the situation changed. The first great post-war recession hit. Capitalism went into slowdown in growth and into recession. Now there was a new consensus—between Geoffrey Howe, the Chancellor of the Exchequer of the Thatcher government, and Denis Healey, the Chancellor of the Exchequer of the Callaghan Labour government. On the three basic issues of full employment, mixed economy and the welfare state, the new consensus was exactly the opposite of the old consensus of Butskellism. Labour said forget about full employment. It was Labour's Jim Callaghan who announced that you cannot keep throwing money at jobs. Now no one talks about full employment. A very high level of unemployment is regarded as both inevitable and 'acceptable', and has been since the late 1970s. When it comes to the mixed economy, the Labour Party has accepted the privatisation that has occurred. Its recent campaign did not talk about buying back electricity, gas or British Telecom. Kinnock made it clear that privatisation would continue, and would not be reversed. So the idea of the mixed economy has been abandoned. And hand in hand with this goes acceptance of a very poor welfare state. It was Labour that closed hospitals, cut education and so on from 1976 at the behest of the IMF. Now the consensus has shifted. This was because between 1945 and 1978 the annual rate of growth of gross national product was 3.1 percent. Since then it has halved; in the last 13 years output in manufacturing rose by less than one tenth a year. Under such conditions there is no possibility of full employment. And there is very little surplus for welfare when billions have to be paid to the unemployed. When the government budget is so tight it is impossible to spend money on nationalising industries, privatisation is a necessary source for paying government expenditure. There is still consensus, but on different terms. There is a consensus of high unemployment, privatisation and welfare cuts. The parties are close together but not identical. They approach the question in different ways, but with many of the same assumptions.

How does that undercut the traditional base for reforms which Labour has relied on since 1945?

It leads to the fundamental problem for social democracy today. What we have is reformism without reforms. Reformist consciousness develops from a major contradiction inside capitalism: the working class must emancipate itself, yet at the same time the prevailing ideas are those of the ruling class. This contradiction exists in reality inside the working class. There are those who always accept the prevailing consciousness, those who completely reject Tory ideology, and those in the middle who both reject and accept it. They resist the prevailing ideology, and believe in change within the system itself. Reformist consciousness wants to change the system but lacks the confidence. At this stage of Labourism it is a period of reformism that doesn't achieve reforms. The level of reforms that capitalism can afford is different in different periods. When capitalism is prosperous it can afford more reforms. But one thing it cannot function without is profit. Therefore if the economy is in crisis one of the two things have to give—either profit or the reforms. The logic of reformist politics is therefore always to move to the right in a period of capitalist crisis. Fritz Tarnow, an ideologue of the German trade unions in the early 1930s, said that capitalism is so sick we have to be the doctors of capitalism. There is a logic in this, because if capitalism is sick it cannot afford reforms.

Not only can you have reformism without reforms, as we have at the moment, but also reformist leaders who, because of the crisis of capitalism, move massively to the right. Under such conditions they become the source of workers' disgruntlement. This is the situation in France at the moment under Mitterrand. In 1981 he got over 50 percent of the vote for the presidency and people celebrated, yet in the elections last March the Socialist Party got 18 percent of the vote and were beaten to third position in Paris, Marseilles and Lyons, coming after the National Front. This shows the scale of workers' disgruntlement with them. The reformist government can become the target. It does not cause the mess that is capitalism, but it becomes the agent of capitalism.

The reformists are also unable to deal with it. They take a moderate position and try to survive. But with the dissatisfaction things can move either to the left or to the right: either it can be directed to the real causes of the trouble—the employers, the state—or it can be directed against blacks or Jews. The reformists cannot deal with it at all, and they cannot mobilise in the right direction. The condition of the reformist party which cannot deliver reforms and creates anger against itself means they are unable to fight back.

What about the role of the trade union bureaucracy and its relationship both to the working class and the Labour leaders? How does this fit into your analysis?

The Labour Party is the political expression of the trade union bureaucracy, which vacillates and mediates between the two main classes, and also between different sections of workers. In the long period of expanding capitalism after the war workers were confident. They knew they could improve their conditions by sectional and even individual activity, something we called at the time 'do it yourself reformism'. Thus you could have reforms, but also apathy. The trade union bureaucracy did not have much pressure on them. The reforms that workers fought for did not amount to a fight against the trade union bureaucracy.

Things changed in the early 1970s. The situation meant that there was generalisation. British capitalism went into crisis, and the economy became a real problem for the government of the day. The Labour government had gone on the offensive over wages and in 1969 tried to introduce *In Place of Strife* to curb the trade unions. This met massive resistance and failed. The Heath government anti-union laws and incomes policy politicised things further. Because the Tories generalised, the workers also generalised. This led to the miners' strikes of 1972 and 1974 and the dockers' strike in 1972 against the Industrial Relations Act. The workers were confident and they met the generalisation of the ruling class head on. The anger was against the Tories, but class conscious workers raised the slogan of a Labour government. That's what we got in 1974. It led to the Social Contract which caused widespread demoralisation. Workers came to the conclusion that all industrial action had to be official in order to win.

The years 1974-79 were the first period that scabbing was official. For example, at Heathrow a strike of 5,000 engineers saw the rest of the workforce, some 60,000 of them, instructed to cross the picket line by their unions. It is important to realise that when workers generalise in their struggle they need an organisation that can also generalise. When workers hesitate then they need people to argue for action. This was not forthcoming from the union bureaucracy and as a consequence there was a growth of both demoralisation and right wing ideas, which in turn eased the election of a Thatcher government in 1979.

Since then the trade union bureaucracy has moved massively to the right. And the rank and file has come to depend very heavily on the bureaucracy. In the Labour Party the union leaders became the fundamental force in pushing through new realism. There is now a new condition of apathy—alienation from mass organisation—which has been a long process. What does this apathy and alienation mean for the future?

It is useful to compare the situation today with that of France in 1968. When the general strike happened there it was like a bolt from the blue. Not even French Marxists could see it coming. It was not seen or predicted because of the real levels of alienation from mass organisation. There are usually a number of barometers to judge workers' consciousness: how many are in the workers' party, the unions, how many come to demonstrations, how many papers do they sell, or read, and how does this compare to the size of the organisation? If there is no barometer then the workers themselves don't know the mood that others feel—the individual is as conscious as his mates. So the struggles and activity that do take place are like sudden outbursts. Of course there is always an immediate catalyst, but the only reason that there is such a level of mass action is because there was so much discontent around. In France for nearly 20 years before 1968 there was a decline in workers' confidence, there was no barometer to judge workers' mood and then suddenly it burst. The activity came, but the action came from nothing, it rose and then it disappeared. There was no mass revolutionary organisation so there was no continuation and we had a right wing government until 1981 when Mitterrand won.

This sort of swing upwards and downwards is absolutely inevitable in such circumstances. The alienation means there is a vacuum, and it can swing in either direction—to the right and the left, and it can swing massively either way.

The difference this time is that we are not going through a period of expanding capitalism. It is not like France after 1968. Capitalism is in world crisis. The Tories' problems continue. I believe the government will be forced to raise taxation, carrying out massive cuts in expenditure. The stress on tightening fiscal policy is clear from the appointment by Major of three Thatcherites—members of the No Turning Back Group—to key ministerial posts: Michael Portillo is Chief Secretary to the Treasury in charge of this year's spending round while Peter Lilly has taken charge of Social Security, the biggest spender, and Michael Howard has Environment, responsible for local government. Unemployment will continue to rise. There is not enthusiastic support for the Tories now, despite the election result. That is likely to worsen. If in a couple of years time the Labour Party comes to office—and of course it still can do so despite what is said, it will do so with very high levels of passivity, and alienation from organisation. Under such conditions a Labour government can open the door to a right swing—as in France—(and Labour will not have the honeymoon period that Mitterrand had). So from the beginning the Labour Party will be part of the problem. It will not be able to solve the anger. Instead it will be the subject of the anger. It will be part of the problem. In this situation the role of the revolutionary party becomes absolutely crucial.

Many people will agree with this analysis but they will draw pes-simistic conclusions from the election result—for example they will argue that we need proportional representation or a pact with the Liberals. The danger is that people will be very angry in the short term, but will then draw very pessimistic conclusions. How do you deal with this?

In terms of the Labour Party as a whole there is no doubt that the main conclusions drawn will be right wing. If Kinnock had won, people would have said it proves that right wing policies are correct, but with Kinnock losing the election they will say it proves that the working class is finished. Maybe the campaign was too aggressive, the Smith budget went too far on tax. One conclusion is to have an alliance with the Liberals. What does this mean? In the south Labour people would not put candidates against the Liberals and in the north the Liberals would not stand against Labour. But the problem is that all the surveys show that the majority of Liberals are more pro-Tory than Labour. So in the south the Labour voters will have no alternative while the Liberals in the north will vote Conservative. The result will be to strengthen the move to the right. The logic of this alliance will be to transform the Labour Party into a party like that of the Democratic Party in the US.

I don't believe this will happen. They can't deliver it, although they can move in this direction. But the relationship with the unions is too strong, and the Liberals hate the unions. Even so, the move towards it can do massive damage to ordinary Labour Party members. The only thing that will stop this drift to the right will be mass action outside the Labour Party. The problem with this however is that you cannot see it coming. There is massive anger in this country, which is resentful—it's not active anger yet, but it is there nonetheless. We can never be sure when this anger will explode.

The problems exist for our side. But look at their side. They will make mistakes—like the poll tax—a stupid arrogant thing from their point of view. In the long term British capitalism faces huge problems because of its many weaknesses. It also has problems now. What will happen exactly in a year or two years time is much harder to see. Because of the anger and the crisis of the system there will be periods of rebellion. We don't know when but there will be. We didn't predict the poll tax riot in Trafalgar Square, but it happened because there was so much anger around. This is still the case today.

There is an argument about structure—that the working class is dead, the decline of the working class, the working class is conservative.

This will get a lot more resonance now as a result of the election. How do you respond to it?

The argument about Essex man is nothing new. In 1959 after Labour lost three general elections there were people who argued, 'Must Labour lose?' And the conclusion they reached was, of course, that they must, because there had been sociological change in the working class. Then they said the working class is mesmerised by television and washing machines. For the Labour Party to win elections it has to sever its ties with the trade unions and purge its constitution of Clause 4 (nationalisation of industry). Thus Douglas Jay, one of the most prominent leaders of the Right in the Labour Party, wrote:

> *The better off wage earners and numerous salary earners are tending to regard the Labour Party as associated with a class to which they themselves do not belong... We are in danger of fighting under the label of the class which no longer exists.*

This 'class which no longer exists' a few years later led massive strikes in the mines, docks, engineering and print, which brought the Heath government to its knees.

When Labour won the 1964 and 1966 elections with a massive majority of some 100—the same people wrote that the Labour Party is the 'natural party of government'. They are completely empirical, so today they forget this history as it is inconvenient for them.

It is not true that a good standard of living for workers will drive them away from Labour. The real question is whether collective action to raise the standard of living or to defend it, or individual actions raise the confidence of the workers. The most militant workers in the First World War were the top wage earners—the skilled engineers of the Clyde, skilled engineers of Germany, Italy. It is not true that the poorest earners are the backbone of the Labour Party. They never have been. On the contrary, often it is the lower paid workers, people in non-union jobs and so on, who lack confidence to fight and to organise. It is not so much their standard of living that determines workers' confidence, and so their consciousness, but whether they are involved in collective action to defend their standard of living.

The key is not the composition of the working class—manual or white collar—but its size and strength. All the experts just look at the surface and draw superficial conclusions. So Labour losing in the 1983 election led to it becoming holy writ that Labour would never ever win because it would need the biggest swing since 1945. Then the polls in the recent campaign showed that Labour was going to win, and so the argument completely disappeared. The so called experts always look to the status quo. The revolutionaries must always look to the potentiality of the working class, not the actuality. When the struggle takes place, in terms of class consciousness workers will know they are workers as part of the same class. Consciousness will come from the struggle.

What about prospects for the left? Do you see a revival for the Labour left in any real sense in the aftermath of the election defeat?

We are not going back to 1981, when the Labour left was at its height with the movement around Tony Benn, and revolutionaries outside the Labour Party were very isolated, for a number of reasons.

Firstly, in 1981 there was an industrial downturn, with job losses and defeats in the workplaces. There was also a political upturn, which took the form of Bennism. There was a real feeling that the Labour Party could be changed from below, and that its ordinary members would have much more say in running it. This feeling does not exist today. Then large sections of the union block vote supported the left. Today the leadership contest, the battle for the leadership for the Labour Party, is between two right wing candidates. The union machine is in the pocket of the right. They will decide between Smith and Gould, not Benn and Smith.

There is a great deal of bitterness and anger around at the roots of the Labour Party. People feel that they allowed Kinnock to move the party to the right because it would pay off electorally, and exactly the opposite has happened. But no one on the left really believes they can transform Labour from below at the moment.

Also in 1981 the Labour left controlled the GLC and 50 other municipal councils. This was the beginning of the period of municipal socialism. The strategy was a disaster. The majority of the Labour left refused to fight over ratecapping in the mid-1980s, and more recently over the poll tax. Now, however, they have to live with the past. These councils are imposing cuts, implementing the poll tax because they refused to fight. This has gutted the Labour left. There is no way at present that the Tony Benn phenomenon could exist through local government. That is not to say that it cannot have influence in say five or ten years time. But for now the councils are not a point of resistance for the left. Likewise the union machine is not a symbol of resistance for the left. Indeed, the union leaders are pushing Labour even further to the right at present. The revolutionary left, therefore, is in a much stronger position than it was in 1981.

There are also wider political questions which have in recent years damaged the case of the Labour left. We have seen reformism in action over the last few years. People say reformism works, but you only have to look to the experience of France, Spain and Australia. They have implemented 'Thatcherite' policies with a vengeance. It is a lot more difficult now to say reformism works, and therefore workers begin to look to other, revolutionary, alternatives. In addition the death of Stalinism, following the events of the past three years in Russia and Eastern Europe, has had a marked impact on Western socialists. In the early 1980s Stalinism was still a world phenomenon. The bulk of the left, even those in the Labour Party, looked to its politics and analysis. Now that has gone. Again that has led some socialists to more right wing conclusions. However, it has also led many to looking round for socialist alternatives to Communism or Labourism. That also means that the world is a much more volatile place now, which gives much greater opportunities to the revolutionary left.

So would you say that it is still possible for revolutionaries to take initiatives and build, or does Labour's defeat and the weakness of the Labour left mean a period of retrenchment? Are there still the opportunities that existed during the last days of Thatcher? What does this mean for the revolutionary party in terms of pushing outwards and the opportunities that exist at the moment?

We live in a period of upheaval. The ruling class, or at least sections of them, will try and put the boot in. We don't know what form resistance will take. But resistance there will be. In every strike members of the SWP must intervene actively. Socialists or the socialist organisation can play a crucial role in every act of resistance—industrial or political.

The party is very important and it is essential that we continue to push outwards. There are tens or even hundreds of thousands of individuals who are looking for solutions to the crisis, to the problems of reformism and to all the other major questions in the world today. We must try to provide some of those answers. So we have an audience for our paper, and for our other publications. But we cannot be complacent. Because there is a low level of struggle at present, because there is a lack of generalisation, we have to pay a great deal of attention to individuals. We must take care of our members, the non-members who are around us and come to our meetings, our *Socialist Worker* readers. We have to do two things simultaneously: look outwards towards the sorts of issues around which we can mobilise people; and look to the base, to our members and to the branches. If we can build a sizeable revolutionary organisation, and continue to deepen our roots in the local working class movements, then we are very well placed for the struggles ahead.

Engels said that our struggle is on three fronts—the economic, the political and the ideological. We should not mechanically separate these things, but they are not exactly the same. Building the

revolutionary party now is crucial. The defeat of Labour opens the door
to the building of the party. Millions of people may feel depressed, but
hundreds of thousands will ask the question why? And we can talk to a
few of these individuals. We can build the party organisation and
present a revolutionary alternative.

Did Lenin lead to Stalin?

ROBERT SERVICE

Very few scholars and commentators nowadays contend that there was an inevitability about the passage from the political, economic and social policies of Lenin to the Stalinist programme of the 1930s and 1940s. Stalin introduced a régime of long term mass terror. Stalin imposed a grotesque and uniform official ideology, ludicrously overstating his own merits—even at the expense of Lenin. He completely rewrote history. Stalin had dictatorial power over his party, his government and the state. He exercised this power with systematic and extreme brutality over a period of more than 20 years. Stalin also brought into direct or semi-direct state ownership every single sector of the economy: trade, agriculture, industry and banking. And Stalin initiated a covert policy of Russian nationalism, spilling over into virulent anti-semitism in the post-war years: the Bolshevik leader from Georgia was the greatest Russian chauvinist of them all.

Undeniably Lenin did much to distance himself from Stalin. In 1922-3, as he lay on his deathbed and composed his political testament, he recommended Stalin's removal from the General Secretaryship of the Russian Communist Party's Central Committee. There can be no clearer indication of the alienation of the founder of the Soviet state from the colleague who directed the party's administrative machinery. No other Politburo member had earned so fierce a criticism from Lenin.

Even so, Lenin by no means suggested that Stalin should be ejected entirely from the party leadership; and he certainly did not propose the expulsion of Joseph Stalin from the party: in the 1920s such a

suggestion would have been inconceivable. Stalin's sins were many in
Lenin's judgement. Yet these did not induce him to seek to terminate
his political career. Nor did Lenin, even on his deathbed, rehearse some
of the nastier elements of Stalin's past—elements that were visible
even in the civil war. When Stalin was on the southern front in mid-
1918, for example, he had encouraged a mass terror and a fundamental
lawlessness that was notorious in the Tsaritsyn region. Lenin had not
disciplined him over that nor did he see fit to include any reproof in his
political testament.

Lenin also had an especially bossy personality. Once he had taken
against someone in a particular matter, he tended to get preoccupied
and even obsessed. His illness aggravated this trait. His spat with Stalin
in 1922-3 over foreign trade, bureaucracy and the federal constitution
made him beside himself with fury against one of the two Bolshevik
leaders whom he identified as his likely successors. A psychological
factor was involved: and only those who like their politics to consist of
the purest saints and entirely irredeemable villains find this an
uncomfortable observation.

Consequently, although much attention is paid to what divided
Lenin and Stalin in those crucial years, we must not overlook what
continued to unite them. The unifying points go unmentioned in the
testament for the precise reason that they were not divisive. Among
them were the belief of both of them in dictatorship; in the one party
state; in the continued deployment of terror whenever the party's power
was thought to be threatened; in the imposition of a single
unchallengeable ideology; in the subjugation of all public institutions
and mass organisations to the will of the party; in the strictest internal
party discipline; in the efficacy of crude political language and
methods; in the need to indoctrinate the working class.

This system of beliefs was in a condition of partial construction
before the October Revolution. The scaffolding for its walls was in
place by the middle of the civil war. The roof was added at the
inception of the New Economic Policy in 1921. The collective architect
was the central and local party leadership, and its major thinker and
planner was Vladimir Lenin.

And what about this Lenin? There is natural sympathy for him in
1922-4. The effort needed to dictate his last thoughts to a group of
secretaries was enormous. After his physical collapse in spring 1922,
he had only residual use of his limbs and his power of speech was
limited; and he was kept isolated in the government sanatorium at
Gorki, tended by several Russian and German doctors and by his wife
Nadezhda and sister Maria. He was dying, and knew it. He was only in
his early fifties. Had disease not struck him down, there was every
reason to expect that he would continue to guide the Bolshevik Party

and Soviet state. What became known as his political testament were words extricated from a still lucid mind by a man determined that he would not leave this life before communicating his worries to party comrades.

No wonder that Gorbachev encouraged professional Soviet historians to accentuate the importance of this last period in Lenin's life. Here was Lenin apparently at his gentlest. Lenin the harrier of Stalin and his cronies. Lenin of the New Economic Policy. Lenin the protector of the peasants. Lenin the advocate of commercial interests and of concessions to private enterprise. Lenin the opponent of bureaucrats and nationalists. Nor was this an image of Lenin which was confined to the Soviet Union. On the contrary, Lenin as the embodiment of Soviet communism with a human face has been a widely, albeit not universally, reproduced picture in the West.

The portrait bears as little relation to reality as Holbein's representation of Anne of Cleves for the delectation of Henry VIII. Lenin, after introducing the New Economic Policy in 1921, by no means rejected terror. Admittedly he narrowed the range of its operations. But certain social categories could expect no mercy. For example, it was in 1922 that he recommended the arrest and execution of Russian Orthodox Church bishops. This was said in the privacy of Politburo discussions. His plan derived not from the revelation of some definite anti-régime plot but rather from a wish to terrorise the clergy into a condition of fear which would last decades.

Cultural controls were tightened under the New Economic Policy. To be sure, there remained much latitude for creative self-expression. The murderously bizarre attempts at monolithism in the 1930s were as yet unimagined. But the New Economic Policy, coming after an exhausting civil war, was used by Lenin to assert the party's general authority in areas of social life previously touched little by him. Thus Lenin was responsible for the expulsion from Soviet Russia of dozens of leading philosophers, poets and novelists in 1922. Lenin in the last phase of his career was far from being a 'liberal' communist in policy for the arts.

Least of all was he liberal towards outright political adversaries. He refused to revoke the ban on internal factions he had imposed at the 10th Party Congress in March 1921. Nothing in his testament indicated a change of mind. Expulsion from the party was his ambition for Alexander Shlyapnikov's Workers' Opposition if the Opposition refused to cease activity. This, however, was mild in comparison with his attitude to non-Bolshevik political opponents. In 1922 he notoriously demanded that the leadership of the Party of Socialist Revolutionaries be arrested, put on trial and executed. Negotiations about the Civil Code in the same year, moreover, demonstrated a readiness to treat the Mensheviks with the same ruthlessness. Only the intervention of his central party colleagues stopped him from acting quite so dictatorially towards rival parties.

But what about Lenin's economic policy in 1921? Certainly he aimed at short term concessions to private enterprise after the civil war. But his projections in the medium term were for increased state intervention, increased state regulation, increased state ownership. The New Economic Policy was only a strategic manoeuvre. Furthermore, Lenin had no realistic answer to the aggravation of bureaucratic problems that any future amassment of state-economic authority would involve.

Nor did Lenin have much practical respect for national self determination. A dispute occurred between him and Stalin over proposals for a federal constitution in 1922. The specific bone of contention was Stalin's wish to deprive his native Georgia of its republican status and push it into a Transcaucasian republic which would seek incorporation in the greater Soviet Union. Lenin, on reflection, demurred but found Stalin reluctant to give way to him. And yet not even in the heat of the controversy did Lenin differ from Stalin in wishing to deny national self determination to the Georgian people. Both took it for granted that the Georgians would be held in the USSR willy nilly. No plebiscite would be held. And the central party leaders in Moscow would ensure Georgian political compliance by maintaining direct control over the Georgian Communist Party. Georgia's subjection to the Kremlin would be sternly enforced.

Lenin's last struggle, then, was certainly the struggle of a dying man who fought right to the end and passed away with dignity. But Lenin also died a Bolshevik; and his Bolshevism contained many genes which were to produce Stalinism in the following decade.

If Lenin had been a fit man and had lived into that decade, the theories and policies and practices of his party would have been different from Stalin's in several basic respects. It over-stretches belief that Lenin would have exterminated his close colleagues or that he would deliberately have sent millions to their deaths in the blood purges of the late 1930s. It cannot be discounted that Lenin too would have resorted to at least some degree of force in introducing collective farming; but Lenin would have been unlikely to have collectivised the peasantry at the expense of the lives of the millions who were either 'de-kulakised' or else reduced to starvation in the early 1930s. And yet Bolshevism itself had a predisposition in favour of political, economic and social ultra-authoritarianism; and, even if not Stalin but Trotsky or Bukharin or even Kamenev had assumed the supreme party leadership after Lenin's death, an ultra-authoritarian system of rule would have prevailed. Trotsky, Bukharin and Kamenev—like Lenin—advocated a milder variant of Bolshevism than Stalin's. But it was still Bolshevism.

Admittedly the Bolsheviks were a party whose members in 1917, among themselves, acted relatively democratically—but their orientation in public policy had never been democratic. Indeed their aim was to establish a dictatorship of the working class and the poorest peasants. It requires naïveté of a specially impervious order to deny that this orientation would corrupt the internal life of both the Bolshevik Party and the new Soviet state. All dictatorship corrupts; but totalist dictatorship, even if it falls short of its planned realisation, corrupts totally.

Thus the degeneration of the October revolution is not attributable exclusively to factors outside the control of the Bolshevik Party leadership. To be sure, the intervention of the Allies in the post-October civil war exacerbated political conflict. And the Reds were not the only perpetrators of terror: the brutality of the Whites was equally ghastly. Furthermore, not all the consequences of the October revolution were foreseen or even forseeable by the Bolsheviks (although the Mensheviks had given them warning about several). Even so, these were not the factors which, above all others, brought about the violent and authoritarian 'excesses' which took place in the former Russian Empire in the Lenin era. There really was something violent and authoritarian both about Bolshevism from its inception after the turn of the century and about the October revolution from its earliest days.

A grievous responsibility must be laid at the door of a handful of leaders such as Lenin, Trotsky and Stalin. They formulated the ideas and consolidated the practices which offered land, peace and workers' control to the mass of the population. They truly believed that a new society was buildable which would benefit all mankind. To them it seemed that the dawn of socialism was about to direct its rays across all Europe. But their utopianism had its overpoweringly dark side; and they also found dictatorship and terror entirely congenial.

Yet these figures were not the whole party. They would not have had such an impact if their assumptions had not been shared by leaders at lower levels of the hierarchy of territorially based committees. The Bolshevik Party in the 1920s, the party of Lenin and Stalin, was guided by ex-undergrounders. Such cadres had endured the persecutions of the Tsarist period. They had emerged as tough and dedicated revolutionaries. They wanted to form not a routinised administration but a dynamic, flexible régime which emphasised action at the expense of procedures. They were legal nihilists. As opposition and difficulties mounted after the October revolution, their trust in dictatorship and in the supreme virtues of their own party was reinforced. Ruthlessness gave way to extreme ruthlessness. By the end of the civil war even those central and local leaders—such as Lev Kamenev's sympathisers—who had had trepidations about this approach to the construction of socialism accepted it as natural and desirable. Consequently Stalin found no need, even at the height of his power in the 1930s and 1940s, to draw up a new party programme to replace the Leninist programme of 1919. Stalin altered much in Lenin's policies. Yet he left the party programme not merely unmodified but absolutely intact. It was not until 1961, under Nikita Khrushchev, that a new programme was ordered to be written. Stalin's apparent indolence is not hard to explicate: the basic tenets of the 1919 programme were totalitarian in aspiration.

This same party was united in its fundamental anti-peasantism. Its notions were deeply attached to urban developments, to large scale organisations, to the industrial proletariat. It was united, too, in a commitment to the speedy promotion of the working class to state administrative posts. In addition, it was united by a determination to stamp on the throat of all other political parties both socialist and non-socialist. Not only that: there were lamentably few Bolshevik leaders at the centre or in the provinces who were reluctant to crush the autonomy of trade unions and factory committees from 1918 onwards. The deep streams of a pre-1917 ultra-authoritarianism welled up to cover a massive flood plain.

It is amazing that anyone in the late 20th century can still believe that the Bolshevik party was quintessentially socialist. A party which could thrust its jackboot into the face of the labour movement, as did the Bolsheviks in their first years of government, has so distorted a conception of socialism that it should no longer be described as socialist.

The people to feel sorry for are not only the workers and soldiers who voted for the Bolsheviks in the local soviet elections of 1917 but also the vast bulk of ordinary Bolshevik Party members. Most of them had read no Marx, seen nothing of Lenin and rarely went to party meetings. Socialism was a vague and ill defined concept for most rank and file Bolsheviks. But such recruits, before the October revolution, cannot be shown to have wanted their party ruling Russia dictatorially and alone. Most evidence suggests that 'the party masses' (as the leaders called them, with characteristic condescension) shared the sort of aspirations that most Russian workers had in 1917. An all party socialist coalition was a priority for them. They also wanted both peace and an extension of workers' rights in factories and mines. Many of them left the party in disgust in 1918-19 or else joined the faction that in 1920-1 became known as the Workers' Opposition.

But the rank and filers were outmanoeuvred. In 1917 they had had influence over policies without fully predetermining them. Quickly thereafter they lost even this influence. The cadres from the emigration and the Tsarist underground tightened their own command in the one party state. These cadres, contrary to the myth sedulously propagated by those such as Trotsky who sought to explain away their own fall from power in the mid-1920s, were not newcomers to prominence in the party. They were the Old Bolsheviks. They were the backbone of the party of Lenin from the revolutionary period.

It was this party that Stalin inherited, after the intra-party political struggles of the 1920s, from Lenin. Of course, Stalin proceeded to introduce features of his own to party affairs. A difference existed between Lenin's party and the faction within it that Stalin eventually led. Stalin wanted to go even further than Lenin in brutalising Russian politics. Stalin wanted to go faster, and he was going to do it at the cost of millions of lives of completely innocent and unsuspecting people. Stalin's personality was also deeply unbalanced by suspiciousness and vengefulness. He not only wanted to get rid of real enemies, he wanted to get rid of potential enemies as well. He accomplished this aim by means of a mass surgical strike involving the deaths of millions. Lenin's wife, Krupskaya, was to confide to a friend in the 1930s that, if Lenin had not died prematurely in 1924, he would have ended up in one of Stalin's prisons.

All this notwithstanding, the régime that would have existed had Lenin lived longer or had been succeeded by Leon Trotsky would still have been extremely grim. It would still have been a régime which had recourse to terror to secure itself in power and to impose its ideology. It would still have been a régime which was a prison for the peoples. It would still have been a régime with an excess of economic nationalisation, to the point of stifling flair, enthusiasm and practicality. It would still have been a régime which found the technological and output gap widening between itself and the major capitalist powers.

The debate as to whether Lenin led to Stalin, taken in narrow terms, is a non-debate. It is akin to one of those mediaeval theological discussions about the number of angels who can stand on a single pin. Few people even in the Middle Ages were exercised by angel enumeration. Similarly, hardly anyone nowadays is seriously contending that, as night follows day, so Leninism was bound to develop into Stalinism. But the matter does not end there. Debate rightly exists over the degree and type of continuities that existed between Leninism and Stalinism; and only the wilfully blind would fail to see that those continuities are very strong indeed. Similarly the disputes about the alternative paths of evolution for the party after Lenin's death—Bukharinism, Trotskyism or Stalinism—have an

importance not to be ignored. But each strategical option was a
Bolshevik one. Each involved journeying down a *cul-de-sac* of history
with no prospect of creating a society without exploitation and
oppression.

In defence of democratic revolutionary socialism

SAMUEL FARBER

David Finkel has shown elsewhere in this issue the various ways in which John Rees's 'In Defence of October' (*International Socialism*, 52, Autumn 1991) seriously mischaracterised the contents of my book *Before Stalinism, The Rise and Fall of Soviet Democracy* (published by Polity in Britain and in paperback by Verso in the USA). For my part, I want to restate some of the key theses and arguments put forward in that work.

Without questioning that there were major qualitative differences between Stalin's and Lenin's rule in Russia, *Before Stalinism* shows that, by the time Stalin came to power, soviet democracy had already disappeared. Basing myself on the abundant and mostly recent scholarship on the early revolutionary period, I showed how by 1921, and certainly by 1923 when Lenin ceased to function as the leader of revolutionary Russia, soviet democracy no longer existed. I provide extensive documentation to support this claim not only in relation to the soviets in the strict sense of the term, but also in regard to the press, the institutions of workers' management and control and the unions.

Here I would like to concentrate on two topics which have been mystified or ignored by many in the revolutionary socialist tradition: the trade unions and socialist legality. In the case of the trade unions, *Before Stalinism* specifically showed how Lenin's defence of trade union autonomy in 1921 was no more than symbolic. By this time the trade unions had already come, through the mechanism of party fraction discipline, under the effective control of the Communist Party. In any event, the Eleventh Party Congress in March and April of 1922, the last in which Lenin actively participated, left little doubt about the meaninglessness of Lenin's proposed union autonomy. This Congress resolved that the secretaries and chairmen of the central committees of the unions must be party members of long standing and that the chairmen, secretaries and members of the leading regional trade union bodies had to be party members of at least three years standing. Furthermore, the Congress decided that party members could be co-opted rather than elected to union office. Finally, it was agreed that all conflicts and frictions on union questions would be resolved by the party and the Comintern rather than by the unions themselves.[1] Finally, the notion that there is no need for trade union autonomy under socialism had been established by the Bolshevik majority at a number of trade union congresses that took place before 1921. In fact, as early as the first trade union congress which met at the end of 1917, Zinoviev, who attended the congress as a representative of the Bolshevik Party, made this very claim as a matter of theory and principle. At that congress Zinoviev made an argument that has since become all too familiar, 'I ask you, why and from whom do you need independence: from your own government...?' He also explicitly rejected the right to strike, arguing along the same lines that 'the strike would be directed against the workers themselves.'[2]

Before Stalinism discusses issues pertaining to socialist legality, a topic that many revolutionary socialists would rather not talk about. At the theoretical level, the book criticises Lenin's inclusion of lawlessness as an intrinsic feature of the 'dictatorship of the proletariat', a term which of course refers to a whole historical period and not merely to the violent days and months during and immediately after the overthrow of the old order. At a more concrete and specific level, *Before Stalinism* examines such matters as the post civil war Criminal Code of 1922 which attempted to legalise arbitrary government. For instance, this code continued to uphold the notion developed during the civil war (1918-20) that an act could be considered a criminal offence even if it was not expressly forbidden by any existing law. In addition, the 1922 code allowed for no procedure equivalent to the right of *habeas corpus* which was meant to ensure that an arrested person was charged and brought before a judge, or else released.[3]

Before Stalinism also examines Lenin's endorsement of collective or categorical punishments, ie terror, during *and well after* the end of the civil war. The term collective or categorical punishment refers to the use of punishment against people who are not even suspected of having been actually involved in carrying out, or helping to carry out, any specific acts against the revolutionary government. Instead, what made these people victims of punishment was that they were thought to share with the possible suspects a common political ideology, party or class membership, or even ethnicity. My book also shows some of the many instances where leaders of the revolutionary government resisted or opposed the use of collective punishments, sometimes even provoking Lenin's anger (eg the Petrograd Bolshevik Central Committee on the occasion of Volodarsky's assassination in June of 1918).[4]

While a student at the LSE from 1961 to 1963 I was a member of the Socialist Review tendency (renamed International Socialism while I was still in London). I still remember our strong arguments against the soviet 'workers' bomb' defended by some Young Socialist comrades. At the time we insisted that the 'workers' bomb' was incompatible with revolutionary socialist principles. Along the same lines, I want to argue that while collective or categorical punishments (terror) are perfectly compatible with petty bourgeois dictatorships (eg Robespierre), let alone capitalist imperialism, fascism or Stalinism, they are by their very indiscriminate nature unacceptable to a workers' state. There is a major and qualitative difference between measures designed to deprive the former ruling classes of their social and economic power (eg confiscation) and the quite different matter of legally penalising people on the basis of group membership and social origins, rather than of particular criminal or political offences committed by specific individuals. The issue here is not one's love or hatred for the former ruling classes, but what all this reveals about the revolutionary government's legal conceptions and the future consequences of this for *all*.

Western Cold War historiography argued that Stalinism was not that different from Leninism and that the authoritarian character of 'Leninism in power' was already built into the original conceptions of Bolshevism as it was developed at the beginning of the 20th century. *Before Stalinism* clearly and unambiguously rejects such an interpretation. Instead my book endorses and articulates the reasons for the October revolution and also emphasises the fundamentally democratic character of that upheaval. In the process, I argue against several of Rosa Luxemburg's criticisms of the Bolsheviks and show, for example, how the suppression of the Constituent Assembly was quite defensible on democratic grounds.

I also put forward the argument that most of the undemocratic practices of 'Leninism in power' developed in the context of a massively devastating civil war and in fact cannot possibly be understood outside such a context. But while the devastation caused by the civil war is a very *necessary* part of the explanation for the decline and disappearance of soviet democracy, it is by no means *sufficient*.

For one thing, the civil war devastation does not explain why the mainstream Bolshevik leadership as a whole made a virtue out of necessity and theorised the undemocratic and dictatorial measures as permanent features of the dictatorship of the proletariat in Russia. This in turn had helped, by the early 1920s, to kill the free and authentic political life of the country, thus depriving soviet society of a variety of possible political defences against the subsequently rising Stalinist monster.

These often programmatic mainstream Bolshevik politics did not just happen 'occasionally' or were simply a matter of 'rhetorical power' as John Rees claims. If Trotsky's *Terrorism and Communism* or Krupskaya's 1923 defence of the crudest forms of book censorship are not in the words of John Rees 'considered analyses of events', what are they then? Lest the reader conclude that these may have been theoretical and political excesses of Trotsky and Krupskaya but not of Lenin, then what are we to make of Lenin's insistence in 1918 that until a German revolution was forthcoming, the soviets should 'study the state capitalism of the Germans, . . . spare *no effort* in copying it and not shrink from *dictatorial* methods to hasten the copying of it.'[5]

Similarly for Lenin's highly undemocratic views (as a rule not justified as temporary measures applying only to the existing situation) as expressed in a wide variety of situations: for example, his reply to the old Bolshevik worker Myasnikov when the latter argued vigorously for freedom of the press in 1921,[6] or Lenin's several pronouncements defending the one party state made during and after the civil war,[7] or Lenin's intervention in the debate over one man management of industry at the time of the Ninth Congress of the Communist Party in 1920. On that particular occasion Lenin in fact argued that whether there was collegial management or individual management on the shop floor was irrelevant to the question of 'how a class governs and what class domination actually is', since

> *the victorious proletariat has abolished property, has completely annulled it—and therein lies its domination as a class. The prime thing is the question of property. As soon as the question of property was settled practically, the domination of the class was assured.*

Furthermore, Lenin claimed that there was 'absolutely *no* contradiction in principle between Soviet (that is, socialist) democracy and the existence of dictatorial power by individuals.' (Lenin's emphasis).[8]

John Rees also suggests that the economics of War Communism (1918-20) was merely a desperate reaction to the terrible economic situation facing the Bolshevik government. *Beyond Stalinism* makes it quite clear that the mainstream Bolshevik leadership did not plan for or anticipate the development of War Communism. However, my book does show that once this policy was adopted, initially as a response to the enormous economic crisis facing the country, the government then made a virtue out of necessity just as it had done with the suppression of democracy in the political realm. This was clearly reflected in the mainstream Bolshevik writings of the period and most notably in Bukharin's idealisation of War Communism in his *The Economics of the Transition Period*, a study claiming to be nothing less than 'the process of the transformation of capitalist society into communist society'.[9] As it developed, War Communism did come to mean a dogmatic and absolutist attempt to suppress money and the market and revert to a 'natural' economy of barter and state administrative commands. This new economic philosophy became so encompassing and widespread that it even affected activities quite unrelated to the feeding and physical survival of the population or to the conduct of the civil war. Thus for example in Petrograd, people in need of legal services were not allowed to have any say over their own attorneys and had to accept the one chosen for them by the state.[10]

It is particularly important to underline that War Communism also signified the end of workers' management, control and trade union autonomy. This however was no obstacle to the mainstream Bolshevik leadership coming to see the widespread bureaucratic nationalisations of War Communism as a great advance towards the communist goal. It is especially noteworthy that while in 1921 the implementation of the New Economic Policy (NEP) of concessions to capitalism was defined by Lenin as a 'retreat', the disappearance of soviet democracy and workers' control was never so regretted by the mainstream Bolshevik leadership. This does not lead me to conclude that Lenin's mainstream leadership had developed a worked out and hardened political philosophy opposed to workers' management, control and trade union autonomy (as was later the case with Stalinism). I do conclude that in the eyes of Lenin and his co-thinkers these were not defining characteristics of socialism and had a decidedly lower priority than the centralised state control that clearly obtained the upper hand during the years of War Communism. In any case, the political pronouncements of the mainstream Bolshevik leadership in the period subsequent to the civil war cannot be reconciled with what one would have expected from a leadership that did see soviet democracy and workers' power at the point of production as being of the essence of socialism. Among other things, a leadership thus committed to socialist democracy would have repeatedly stressed the temporary nature of the repressive and undemocratic measures *and* would have spelled out the specific conditions and possible time frames for their removal.

However, my critique of what I have termed 'mainstream' Bolshevism is by no means applicable to the whole of Bolshevism. If anything, my whole book could be seen as a brief in support of Victor Serge's often quoted observation that Bolshevism contained a mass of other germs other than the germ of Stalinism. As mainstream Bolshevism developed new politics in the context of civil war conditions, this was opposed by both the early left oppositionists, (workers opposition, democratic centralists) and right oppositionists (Riazanov, Lozovsky) inside the Communist Party. As a matter of fact, practically all my specific criticisms of 'Leninism in power' were made *at the time* by one or another revolutionary and most notably by the early Left and Right Bolshevik oppositions. Therefore, John Rees and the Socialist Workers Party leadership's quarrel is as much with the critique of those Bolshevik opposition groups as it is with my own.

> *Marx's statement about the democratic nature of the socialist movement . . .*
> *and Lenin's, that revolutionary social democracy represents 'the Jacobins*
> *indissolubly connected with the* **organisation** *of the proletariat' are*
> *definitely contradictory. A conscious, organised minority at the head of an*
> *unorganised mass of the people suits the bourgeois revolution, which is,*
> *after all, a revolution in the interests of the minority. But the separation of*
> *conscious minority from unconscious majority, the separation of mental and*
> *manual labour, the existence of manager and foreman on the one hand and*
> *a mass of obedient labourers on the other, may be grafted on to 'socialism'*
> *only by killing the very essence of socialism, which is the collective control*
> *of the workers over their destiny.*[11]

The fact that the mainstream Bolshevik leadership made a virtue out of the anti-democratic necessities imposed by the enormous hardships of the civil war did not develop in an ideological and political vacuum. Instead, this constituted the exacerbation of a Jacobin *aspect* of Bolshevik politics that became dominant under the stimulus of the civil war crisis.

I would contend that pre-civil war Leninism had two sides that were at odds with each other. On one side was the clearly democratic Lenin who always insisted on the close connection between the struggle for democracy and the struggle for and democratic content of socialism. In fact I believe that Lenin had a better understanding than any of his revolutionary socialist contemporaries of the importance of political democracy as a political goal to be pursued by the workers' movement on behalf of society as a whole. This in contrast to other revolutionary socialists (sometimes including Rosa Luxemburg) who for reasons of economism, workerism or a schematic economic determinism derided the political struggle for general democratic demands such as the right of nations to self determination.

Yet, alongside this emphasis on the struggle for democracy, Lenin and his co-thinkers also held a number of essentially Jacobin ideas particularly in regards to *revolution*. Or, speaking more precisely, a quasi-Jacobin view since Lenin, unlike petty bourgeois Jacobinism, was committed to rooting the revolutionary movement in the politically organised working class. The Jacobin element in this quasi-Jacobinism refers to a heavy emphasis on the will and dedication of the activist minority as contrasted with the weight of *institutions* that encompass that minority as well as much broader sectors of the working class and population as a whole. It is also useful to recall in this context Lenin's repeated tendency, noted in *Before Stalinism*, to solve grave political problems through the appointment of what he considered to be good reliable individuals to positions of power (eg in the Cheka) rather than through the carrying out of structural institutional changes. Similarly, Lenin often tended to see, as in the case of the governmental reforms he proposed towards the end of his rule, the democratisation of socio-economic life solely in terms of promoting leaders and office holders with working class and peasant backgrounds without placing equal emphasis on democratic mechanisms that would make these newly promoted leaders institutionally responsible to popular constituencies. The key problem with Lenin's quasi-Jacobin approach was that the working class, unlike the bourgeoisie, can exercise power in society only *democratically* and *collectively* through institutions such as soviets and factory committees. Thus classical Jacobinism could develop dictatorial power without fundamentally affecting the social or economic power that the bourgeoisie held as *individuals*. However, the moment the working class is deprived of democratic control over the institutions through which it exercises power in society, that working class has lost its power, period.

The Jacobin conception of revolutionary leadership is also incompatible with working class power. To the extent that there exists a Jacobin belief that the truth of the revolutionary activists' vision is sufficient guarantee of their authority to act, to that extent the actions of revolutionary leaders cannot be corrected or reversed by representative popular institutions such as the soviets. This Jacobinism becomes even more dangerously anti-democratic when combined with Hegelian sounding notions such as Trotsky's allusion to the 'revolutionary birthright of the party'[12] in 1921 or the very similar and no less pernicious idea that 'History', in its inevitably progressive development, has reserved *the* role of revolutionary leadership to a particular party or political formation.

While political parties are necessary since they provide indispensable leadership and formulate alternative choices and programmes, it is the representative institutions rather than the parties that must in the last analysis be the repositories of working class and popular sovereignty. From this it follows that the representative institutions must have the ability to *replace* the party in power. While recognising that this would have been, from a practical point of view, a quite difficult task in the conditions of Russia in the early 1920s, I want to stress that the quasi-Jacobin side of Lenin's politics, which became dominant after 1918 and especially after 1921, weighed heavily against his even considering such a possibility *in principle*.

The Jacobin tradition, besides having a strong and uncritical tendency to favour centralisation for its own sake, is not inclined to support the defence of minority rights and civil liberties. While *Before Stalinism* argues that there are of course situations (eg in a civil war) where civil liberties may have to be restricted on a temporary basis, it insists that there can be no real socialist democracy, or for that matter full and genuine innovation and progress, with dissident individuals and minorities terrorised into silence and conformity, and forcefully prevented from attempting to become the new majorities. Today any democratic revolutionary socialism worthy of its name must at the very least cease to regard the defence of civil liberties and the rights of political minorities, both before and after the revolution, as being merely a liberal, let alone 'petty bourgeois', concern.

I began to work on the project that became *Before Stalinism* in 1984, one year before Gorbachev came to power and, of course, before the breakdown of Stalinism and the Soviet Union. I had no inkling that the work I was embarking on would acquire a special relevance within just a few years.

My interest in going back to the 1917-24 period in Russia was a response to political phenomena that had surfaced in the 1970s and early 1980s. On one hand the development of Eurocommunism in Western Europe and on the other hand the rise of a rather distinctive East European and especially Polish dissident political thought which became very prominent after the rise of Solidarity in 1980. These two quite different political traditions coincided in claiming that not only Stalinism but revolution itself was antithetical to democracy. The East Europeans in particular, including people with roots in revolutionary Marxism such as Adam Michnik and Jacek Kuron, borrowed from Karl Popper's idea that the attempt to reshape society as a whole, especially if there is violent action involved, was itself totalitarian. Consequently, democracy was only compatible with peaceful and piecemeal reform. It was hardly surprising that the Russian Revolution was the paradigmatic example chosen by East European dissidents attempting to prove the validity of Popper's dictum. The Eurocommunists for their part also came to the conclusion that they would have to drop Russian 'Leninism' (by which they meant revolution) in order to prove themselves true democrats.

I wanted to demonstrate the compatibility of revolution and democracy. In trying to answer Eurocommunists and East Europeans and taking a closer look at the origins and development of the Russian Revolution I re-examined an explanation for the degeneration of the revolution I had never found fully convincing. I am referring to the views of the left Shachtmanite 'bureaucratic collectivist' tradition and to the British Socialist Workers Party tradition as developed in the 1970s and 1980s. These two traditions, while correctly emphasising the heavy weight of objective factors such as the impact of the civil war and economic collapse, had greatly underestimated the political and ideological sides. The purposes, specific political choices and changes in the political orientation of the main political actors involved had for all intents and purposes been ignored.

I also discovered that these two traditions had unwittingly created a Lenin who was only in part the real historical Lenin. Thus, for example, I found that the very points emphasised by Hal Draper—socialism from below and the importance of political democracy and civil liberties were a lot closer to the early right and left Bolshevik oppositions than to mainstream Leninism. Similarly, I discovered other things that I had never been taught by either tradition; for example, that in 1923, the last year of his life, Lenin had significantly moved in the direction of 'socialism in one country' without of course reaching the extreme of adopting Stalin's later political line.

The collapse of Stalinism, the Soviet Union and most of the worldwide Communist movement has helped to create a radically new situation for the international left. We now find ourselves in a political situation with features similar to the collapse of the Second International in the years subsequent to 1914. As a result, we are confronted with the task of reorganising the left, a task that we should try to help carry out on the basis of building a new democratic and revolutionary socialism.

I hope that *Before Stalinism* offers the elements of a usable past and will make its small contribution to the rethinking of past revolutionary experiences, a necessary task in this process of reorganisation. In particular we cannot ignore the scepticism and pessimism that the failure of Stalinism has created everywhere. The right wing slogan 'No more experiments' has had a powerful appeal in the post-Stalinist Eastern Europe. We cannot respond to such a political climate with evasions and Karl Marx's warnings against utopian blueprints—quite justified in the political climate of his day, but today conveying the message that we simply don't have answers to the tough questions that legitimately trouble people.

We know now that a socialist revolution can be lost in more than one manner or fashion. Not only can the revolution be lost to the counter-revolutionary restorationists wanting to re-establish the old order, it can also be lost to a perhaps less obvious but no less devastating counter-revolution—namely, those supporting a new order devoid of democratic control from below unavoidably opening the road for the formation of a new type of ruling class. This can come about because in following the maxim, 'Hold on to power no matter what', power may indeed be retained, but in order to maintain a type of society radically different from the one the revolutionaries had originally fought for.

A socialist revolution in an advanced industrial country may encounter many of the same objective difficulties faced by revolutionary Russia. We cannot assume that a revolutionary takeover will not be preceded by massive destruction, and we certainly cannot expect the ruling classes in industrialised capitalist societies to hand over a carefully preserved intact economy to the revolutionary opposition. Given this and the ever present possibility of civil war, Lenin's challenge to Gorky to present alternative criteria for determining which blows delivered by a revolutionary government were necessary and which blows were superfluous is as relevant today as it was then.[13] I hope *Before Stalinism* can help us to think of how to meet Lenin's challenge.

I would like to conclude this essay by recalling the spirit of the *Socialist Review/International Socialism* tendency with which I am glad to have been associated in the early 1960s. This was a serious, militant and hard working group that with its humility and lack of dogmatism differed dramatically from practically all the other revolutionary groups that I have known in the subsequent 30 years. Least of all did this group suffer from the political obsession of 'hardness', ie the tough macho 'bolshevik' posturing counterposed to the equally obsessive political 'softness' of social democracy. The SR/IS tendency was also animated by a fresh and creative political spirit that expressed itself in its willingness to engage in a vigorous revolutionary revisionism, eg Tony Cliff on Lenin's theory of the labour aristocracy and on Trotsky's theory of permanent revolution, and Michael Kidron on imperialism. This is the sort of political openness, freshness and flexibility that is necessary in the present period—a period of great crisis for the left but also of great opportunities for those who have new and constructive directions to propose.

At that time Tony Cliff also had a lot to say about the Russian Revolution and its degeneration, and what he said was not contained within the boundaries of Trotskyist or Leninist orthodoxy. I am thinking in particular about the article 'Trotsky on Substitutionism' (*International Socialism*, 2, Autumn 1960), or the book *Rosa Luxemburg* (published as a double issue of *International Socialism* in 1959). The readers of this journal can and will judge for themselves, but I have the strong feeling that what Cliff wrote then is closer to my *Before Stalinism* than to John Rees's 'In Defence of October'.

Notes

1   I Deutscher, *Soviet Trade Unions. Their Place in Soviet Labour Policy* (London and New York, 1950), p65, and Jay B Sorenson, *The Life and Death of Soviet Trade Unionism 1917-1918* (New York, 1969), pp170-71.

2   I Deutscher, op cit, p21, and SA Smith, *Red Petrograd. Revolution in the Factories 1917-1918* (Cambridge, England), p218.

3   I Lapenna, 'Lenin, Law and Legality', in L Schapiro and P Reddaway (eds), *Lenin, The Man, the Theorist, the Leader, a Reappraisal* (New York, 1967), p261, and J Hazard, *Settling Disputes in Soviet Society. The Formative Years of Legal Institutions* (New York, 1960), p314.

4   V I Lenin, letter to Zinoviev, Lashevich and other members of Central Committee, 26 June 1918, in *Collected Works*, Vol 35, February 1912-December 1922 (Moscow, 1966), p336. (Lenin's emphasis.)

5   V I Lenin, ' "Left Wing" Childishness and the Petty-Bourgeois Mentality', *Collected Works*, Vol 27 (Moscow, 1965), p340.

6   V I Lenin, 'A Letter to G Myasnikov', 5 August 1921, in *Collected Works*, Vol 32, December 1920-August 1921, pp504-9.

7   See, for example, the citations in EH Carr, *The Bolshevik Revolution*, Vol 1 1917-1923 (London, Pelican Books), p236.

8   C Sirianni, *Workers' Control and Socialist Democracy. The Soviet Experience* (London, Verso Editions and New Left Books, 1982), p216, and SA Smith, op cit, p228. (Lenin's emphasis.)

9   Cited in SF Cohen, *Bukharin and the Bolshevik Revolution. A Political Biography. 1888-1938* (Oxford, 1980), p87.

10   E Huskey, *Russian Lawyers and the Soviet State. The Origins and Development of the Soviet Bar, 1917-1939* (Princeton, 1986), pp59-61.

11   T Cliff, *Rosa Luxemburg* (London, 1986), p49.

12   I Deutscher, op cit, p55.

13   M Gorky, *Days with Lenin* (New York, 1932), pp44-45.

Defending 'October' or sectarian dogmatism?

DAVID FINKEL

John Rees's lead essay titled 'In Defence of October' (*International Socialism*, 52) could have been a useful contribution. Sadly, in his 'defence' of the revolutionary tradition Rees winds up doing violence to it. For one thing, his rigid recitation of what he takes to be Marxist 'orthodoxy' surprisingly does more to verify than refute the logic of an inevitable totalitarian outcome of the Russian Revolution. (Rees is quite likely oblivious of this implication of his argument, to which I will briefly turn later.)

What is much worse, however, is Rees's systematic violation of the first principle of revolutionary polemics: *that it is obligatory to present and refute other points of view accurately and honestly—particularly opposing views that are also within the revolutionary camp.* In Rees's article the arguments of non-revolutionary or even reactionary authors are accurately stated, because Rees's orthodoxy is adequate to answer them. When it comes to a different *revolutionary* perspective, however, Rees engages in a systematic falsification, despite or rather *because* of the fact that it is the closest to his own.

The perspective I am referring to is that of Sam Farber's book *Before Stalinism, The Rise and Fall of Soviet Democracy.*[1] Rees's 'In Defence of October' includes a running polemic against Farber's perspective. To demonstrate the blatant falsification on Rees's part of what Farber actually wrote admittedly will make tedious reading and comrades are forewarned that they may wish to skip the exercise. This is perfectly OK; the time would be better spent in any case actually reading Farber's excellent book. But I think there is at least some small value in documenting the abuse and reflecting on its cause.

Reference 1: Rees begins by citing recent works by the right wing historian Richard Pipes, the British left wing historian Eric Hobsbawm, the South African Stalinist Joe Slovo—all of whose views are cited clearly enough so you know what they are talking about—and *New Left Review* editor Robin Blackburn, who is quoted in a fragment so that you can't really tell whether or not Blackburn is 'for' the October revolution.[2]

Then follows Rees's first reference to Farber: 'In *Before Stalinism* American socialist Sam Farber argues that Lenin's views and actions *"inevitably and necessarily* led to an elitist form of government" and that the "Bolsheviks firmly adopted policies that moved them a considerable distance towards what later became the Stalinist totalitarian model."'[3] The reference is to pages 99 and 109 of Sam's book. Clearly Sam is in the Bolshevism-led-to-Stalinism camp. Right?

For one thing, Rees shows little interest in the substantial distance, carefully noted by Farber, between a merely 'elitist form of government' and the 'Stalinist totalitarian model'. But Rees's distortion proves really shocking when you actually check the references. Farber writes, in regard to Bolshevik policies on freedom of the press: 'Thus, it was only after the end of the civil war that Lenin and the Bolsheviks firmly adopted policies that moved them a considerable distance towards what later became the Stalinist totalitarian model.'[4] To say the least, this alters the meaning somewhat: here and elsewhere Farber stresses *political choices* made by the Bolsheviks, and the fact that many of these were made after the desperate pressure of civil war had receded. And the deletion of the clause 'it was only after...' changes this passage's whole meaning.

Maybe Rees innocently overlooked this subtlety. Let's look at Farber: '[Lenin's] post-civil war views and actions on freedom of the press and other democratic questions *inevitably and necessarily* led to a thoroughly elitist form of government.'[5] The same distortion is *repeated*: Farber's explicit specification of the period after the civil war as a focus of critical political analysis is deleted by mutilating the quotation. Can this happen twice by mistake?

The point is important, because for Rees's wooden orthodoxy, political choices made after the civil war are basically irrelevant inasmuch as the 'working class base of the workers' state...had disintegrated'[6] in the war. This makes it impossible in his frame of reference to answer Farber's argument, and thus inconvenient to accurately quote it. (More on this below.)

Reference 1a: Immediately following this butchery Rees attempts a clumsy amalgam: 'The same sort of argument has surfaced among oppositionists in Eastern Europe. Adam Michnik "criticised the 'totalitarian temptation' of those activists in Polish Solidarity who wanted the movement to...struggle for state power."' The reference is to Farber, p12. The ordinary reader will assume Sam is quoting Michnik favourably; in fact Sam is sharply critical of the anti-revolutionary political philosophy of Michnik, of whom Sam says 'he has come to see radical political change as somehow totalitarian.' *Because* Farber believes that Solidarnosc *should* have struggled for power in 1981, and that the Bolsheviks were *right* to take power in 1917 (see Farber, p61, for Sam's real views on October 1917), Rees seems to feel compelled to distort him on both points.

Reference 2: After a cogent, orthodox and correct recitation of the reasons why the Bolshevik led revolutionary seizure of power was necessary and justified (Rees is quite competent wherever no original thinking is needed), Rees launches into a discussion on 'The Bolsheviks: A Monolithic Party?'[7] He quotes Stephen Cohen ridiculing the evil genius theory of Lenin's all powerful leadership, then makes this reference to Farber:

> *The left used to set its face firmly against what Cohen calls this 'malignant and straight line' theory. Now, however, things have changed. Sam Farber connects Lenin's attitude to legality in the early Soviet state, which he defines as one of 'expediency at best and of contempt at worst,' with 'Lenin's chronic distaste for codified rules, legal or otherwise.' This attitude, Farber says, 'had sometimes played an important role in his political practice concerning internal party organisation.' This lack of respect for 'rules' and 'legality' helped pave the way for Stalin.*

The reference is to Farber, pp149-150, where we find what Sam actually says, which needs to be quoted in full because it involves a complex point. In his chapter 'Socialist Legality', Sam is critically reviewing some of Lenin's theoretical writings on the meaning of the dictatorship of the proletariat as 'unrestricted by any laws' (Lenin's own phrase), then continues:

> *In practice, however, Lenin on more than one occasion insisted on the strict observance of revolutionary legality [example cited from November 1918]. Ironically, it was the introduction of NEP and the need to provide a degree*

*of security to **capitalists** that later brought about Lenin's greatest degree of emphasis on legality. In sum, it seems that his attitude was that of expediency at best and of contempt at worst. It should be noted that Lenin's chronic distaste for codified rules, legal or otherwise, had sometimes played an important role in his political practice concerning internal party organisation.*

Examples are then cited from old factional battles between 1903 and 1909. Obviously, this has *nothing* to do with the caricature that Rees is supposedly arguing against, that the Bolsheviks were some kind of monolithic party or leadership cult. Farber's real point here and elsewhere is the lack of a systematic theorisation of revolutionary democracy, legality and rights in the Bolshevik legacy. Undoubtedly, the relationship of the internal organisation of any revolutionary leadership (be it the Bolsheviks, Sandinistas, etc) before taking power with its practice once in power is a hugely complicated issue. Many socialist writers have written seriously on the subject—among others Marcel Liebman—but not Rees. The only point of this reference is to score a stupid debater's point that Farber's characterisation of Lenin's party is to the right of the liberal Cohen's, requiring another mutilated quotation.

Reference 3: Regarding the dissolution of the Constituent Assembly, Rees cites arguments by Kautsky, Blackburn and Tim Wohlforth denouncing this action, then states:

*Sam Farber is half willing to defend the Bolsheviks, but '**only if we assume** that their arguments in defence of the soviet system...represented a genuine long term commitment to that alternative form of democratic government.' Yet this is precisely what Farber is **not** willing to assume since his whole book is supposed to demonstrate that the Bolsheviks failed to show any such commitment. Sam Farber too [ie like Robin Blackburn] quotes Rosa Luxemburg, whose criticism of the Bolsheviks' dissolution of the Constituent Assembly is cited by right wingers who would never dream of endorsing any other word that she wrote.*[8]

The reference is to Farber, p56, where Sam writes, 'The Bolshevik rationale for the dissolution of the Constituent Assembly would have been justified from a revolutionary-democratic point of view *only if* [passage as quoted by Rees].' Miraculously, Rees has for once quoted without blatant distortion. He quickly makes up for this, however. First, he fails to mention Farber's detailed *justification* of Bolshevik arguments against the unrepresentative character of the Constituent Assembly. Second, there is Rees's stupid amalgam of anyone who cites Rosa Luxemburg's criticism with 'right wingers who would never dream of endorsing any other word that she wrote'. Third, contrary to Rees's implication Farber *does not endorse*, and in fact sharply criticises, most of Luxemburg's argument against the Bolsheviks on this point.[9] I don't have room to quote here, but part of my purpose will be served if comrades actually read it for themselves.

Reference 4: This comes in Rees's section on 'The Civil War and the White Terror,' and is tied up with Rees's running attempt to create an amalgam of the South African Stalinist Joe Slovo (who throws Trotsky in the same pot with Stalin, a now standard smear), Robin Blackburn (who now believes, if I understand him correctly, that the October Revolution was historically premature and a mistake), and Sam Farber. The underlying purpose of this amalgam is hardly to 'defend October'—if it were, Rees would use Farber's work as that of an ally, not an opponent—but to show the reader that *only* the British Socialist Workers Party (SWP) and its international satellite groups are left to defend the Russian Revolution.

Rees tells us that, 'For many writers it was in this period of War Communism that the first seeds of Stalinism were sown.'[10] (There is a good reason why many writers say this, namely that it is clearly true. In fact the statement should be criticised for its banality, not heresy.) Slovo and Blackburn are duly quoted, then:

> *Sam Farber is happy to repeat Robert C Tucker's designation of this period as 'Stalinist Leninism' and then goes on to argue: 'The governmental euphoria with war communism also implicitly revealed the political and ideological priorities of mainstream Bolshevism. Thus, while this set of policies greatly expanded the powers of the central state and vigorously attempted to reduce the role of the market, at the same time it not only consolidated the Red Terror but for all intents and purposes eliminated workers' control of industry and democracy in the soviets. Again there is no evidence indicating that Lenin or any mainstream Bolshevik leaders lamented the loss of workers' control or of democracy in the soviets...'[11]*

The reference is to Farber, p44. Since we are by now suspicious of what Rees may have left out, we turn to the page and see how Sam finishes that sentence: '...or at least referred to these losses as a retreat, as Lenin declared in connection with the replacement of war communism by NEP in 1921'—a significant point in the argument, since the question at hand is whether the Bolsheviks made voluntarist virtue out of material necessity during War Communism! And Sam continues: 'In fact, as we shall see in the next chapter, the very opposite is the case, eg Lenin defended one-man management as perfectly compatible with socialism.' Rees can't refute these facts, but he can simply delete them.

Farber's citation from Robert C Tucker is instructive in its own right:

> *In fact, Robert C Tucker has referred to this period as 'Stalinist Leninism,'*
> *by which he meant not just the hegemony of certain general ideas and*
> *systems of political belief, but the 'ingrained habits of mind, ways of*
> *defining and responding to situations, styles of action, common memories,*
> *mystique, etc that collectively constitute the culture of a political movement*
> *in so far as a given age cohort of its membership (and leadership) is*
> *concerned... The heritage of that formative time in the history of Soviet*
> *culture was martial zeal, revolutionary voluntarism and* **elan**, *readiness to*
> *resort to coercion...* [I am truncating the quote here for space—DF] *and no*
> *small dose of that Communist arrogance (***komchvanstvo***) that Lenin later*
> *inveighed against.*[12]

For Rees the *content* of all this is irrelevant; only the provocative phrase 'Stalinist Leninism' is useful because lifted out of context it serves the purposes of his amalgam.

Compared to Farber or for that matter Tucker, Rees's own argument is strikingly threadbare. The 'subjective factor' (conscious political choices) was for Rees crucial only in the arena of the European Revolution. But inside Russia in the civil war, 'the limits of action were reduced to withstanding, under ever narrowing constrictions, a siege... It is a tribute to the power of the Bolsheviks' politics and organisation that they took the measures necessary and withstood the siege for so long.'[13] Those who refuse to accept this rather sweeping proposition without question, who seek to subject the Bolsheviks' 'ideological inebriation' (Farber's phrase) with War Communism to serious analysis, are targets for Rees's abuse.

Reference 4a: Immediately below the foregoing, Rees issues forth with the following wisdom:

> *Sam Farber cheerfully brandishes his desire to concentrate on the political,*
> *and criticises others who see 'the question of democracy as if it was in some*
> *way derivative of economics.' Presumably, in this schema, 'democracy' is*
> *equally possible under starving, plague ridden feudalism as it is under 20th*
> *century capitalism.* [Who is actually stupid enough to believe that—or more
> to the point, to believe that anyone else would believe it? DF] *In Sam*
> *Farber's analysis of the civil war we are blankly told that 'the atrocities*
> *carried out by the White Terror are assumed to be given.' Yet this is what*
> **cannot** *be assumed to be given. If we do not give a full account of the*
> *economic crisis, the international situation and the depth of the White*
> *Terror how can we be expected to judge how far the Bolsheviks acted from*
> *necessity? How can we assess the force of circumstance?*

The reference is to Farber, p117. It would appear that Farber lightly brushes off the White Terror and the economic crisis. To get the full flavour of this Really Big Lie, you have to see what Sam actually wrote. The quoted phrase about democracy and economics does not appear at all in the cited passage! I had to find it on p3 of Sam's introduction: In 'the absence of a *theory of revolutionary democracy* [my emphasis—DF] these [socialist and Marxist analyses of the economics of the transition to socialism] tend to deal with the question of democracy as if it was in some way derivative from the economics, if not altogether irrelevant.' Obviously this has nothing to do with some idiotic notion, attributed by implication to Sam by Rees, that democratic institutions could be organised independent of material conditions.

What Farber *does* on p117 is, first, to quote W H Chamberlin on the horrors of the civil war and the counter-revolutionary (White) massacres in particular, and then to say:

Nevertheless, my main concern here is not the total **number** *killed by both sides, shocking as these figures are. Instead, my purpose is to analyse the actions carried out by the Bolshevik leaders...focus[ing] on the political control over the repressive agencies of the revolutionary regime and the criteria guiding the latter's work in such matters as choice of victims and types and severity of punishment. The atrocities carried out by the White Terror are assumed to be given in this context, and are thus of interest only insofar as they may be said, in given instances, to justify or not justify the particular tactics carried out by the Red Terror. From this vantage point, several features of the Red Terror are extremely troublesome and indeed highly disturbing.* [Analysis of Cheka procedures follows.]

The reader will note that Rees's truncated quotation is a cynical manipulation, complete with omission of Sam's explicit phrase 'in this context'. Rees now proceeds to compound the slander with:

Reference 4b: On page 53, in the midst of a lengthy discussion of the civil war, White atrocities and Red Terror, Rees tells us that an 'example often used by right wing historians is based on Cheka leader Latsis' 1918 claim that whether a suspect was capitalist or a worker was enough to determine their guilt or innocence. He went on to urge, "Don't search the records for whether someone's revolt against the Soviet was an armed or only a verbal one." Sam Farber quotes Latsis, but does not bother to quote Lenin's angry rebuttal in which he said that "one need not go to the same absurd lengths as Comrade Latsis."'

We are therefore to believe that Farber has smeared Lenin with the brush of Latsis. But Rees doesn't give a page reference to Farber's book—since Farber 'does not bother to quote' Lenin. So search through Sam's book to page 121, locate the quote from Latsis, and read Sam's *very next sentence*: 'Latsis' comments provoked widespread criticism from a variety of Bolshevik leaders including Lenin.' Guess why Rees omitted the page reference!

Had enough? So have I, which is why I am going to omit most additional examples. But I must add just one more.

Reference 4c: On pages 57-58 of his article Rees recounts the horrifying tortures practised on Bolshevik prisoners by the Makhno and Antonov ('Green') partisans, and the Red Army reprisals, then throws in: 'Characteristically, Sam Farber mentions the shootings [by the Red Army] but not the pardons, the Red Terror but not the Green Terror.' No specific reference is given, but Rees is generally referring to pp122-124 of Farber. On page 122 Farber quotes the scholarly historian Oliver H Radkey, who wrote 'our impression is that there was an excess of torture on the side of the Greens, an excess of killing on the side of the Reds—battle deaths excluded.' Thus in this case Rees has not only falsified Farber's supposed omission, but gratuitously so; the reference is tangential to his argument, and its only point to smear Sam Farber once more.

What remains to be asked is, what is Rees's problem anyway? Why can't the editor of *International Socialism*, to say nothing of seven other British SWP leaders cited for their helpful contributions to the article manage to quote another revolutionary socialist without repeated flagrant misrepresentation?

The sneering tone of Rees's references to Farber's *Before Stalinism*, combined with the above documented falsifications, indicates strongly that Rees wants his readers to dismiss the book without reading it. If *Before Stalinism* is just one more trashing of the October Revolution, reading it is indeed hardly worth the trouble. I suggested above that the British SWP needs to present itself as the *only* remaining defender of October. And there are, I believe, two reasons behind this impulse:

(a) First and most obvious is simple sectarianism. The SWP is driven by the need to claim a unique revolutionary purity as the basis for its 'international tendency'.

(b) Less obvious, perhaps, I detect a lack of confidence on Rees's part in the orthodoxy he is defending. It is as if the entire 'defence of October' depends on upholding the Bolsheviks' correctness at every significant moment, aside from purely tactical matters. This is a brittle orthodoxy indeed: it seems to say that if at any point there were *principled violations of revolutionary democracy* by Bolshevism in power up to (say) the early NEP, the whole case for the revolution may crumble.

As historical analysis this is of course absurd, but it does have its own logic—as a kind of theology. And I can see where the fear of critical questions arises from Rees's own argumentation, which can be summarised as follows: everything the Bolsheviks did was not only 100 percent correct but in essence unavoidable, from organising the seizure of power, through War Communism, to the crushing of Kronstadt, banning of factions and the introduction of NEP. Everything depended on the European revolution. With its failure the Russian workers' state was as if suspended in mid-air; the Russian working class itself was practically dissolved. 'The secret of the Stalinist bureaucracy's success lay in the devastation and isolation of the workers' state.'[14]

Obviously there is truth in all this, as an elementary recitation of the material constraints on the Russian Revolution. But Rees cannot afford to ask himself a deeper level question: if the failure of the European revolution made *socialism* in Russia impossible, as we would all agree, was *Stalinism* then inevitable?

If the answer is 'no', then Rees would have to inquire what kind of politics in the early post-revolutionary years might have improved the chances of a successful social and especially working class resistance to Stalinism, a challenge for which SWP orthodoxy is unprepared. Even if we cannot reasonably condemn Bolshevism for failing to anticipate the literal *destruction of a world revolutionary movement and tens of millions of human lives under the leadership of Stalinism*, we ourselves don't have the right not to ask what lessons might be learned from the pre-Stalin period.

But if the answer is 'yes', then Rees's argument becomes: without European revolution, Bolshevism *did* lead straight to Stalinism. And then it is hard to resist the arguments of a Kautsky or a Blackburn, *was that gamble worth the risk*? Wasn't the October Revolution indeed disastrously 'premature' if its failure to *immediately* spread made a catastrophic *destruction of socialist politics on a world scale for many decades inevitable*?

If Rees were seriously interested in engaging the arguments of Sam Farber, then instead of falsifying them he could have chosen to cite Sam's book as *strengthening* the case for the October Revolution, despite his differences with Sam's harsh criticism of Bolshevik policy. Or he could have left it alone. Instead he felt impelled to treat it as a threat.[15]

All this tells us a sad story about *International Socialism*'s ability to confront arguments *inside* the revolutionary camp honestly. Such practices cannot fail to have negative consequences, not the least of which are the sectarian mis-education of valuable cadres and the high percentage loss of those cadres when they confront, in the real world, questions that the orthodoxy has not prepared them to answer.

Notes

1   S Farber, *Before Stalinism, The Rise and Fall of Soviet Democracy* (Polity Press, 1990).
2   Blackburn's lengthy article 'Socialism After the Crash' appears in *NLR* 185, Jan/Feb 1991 and in his anthology *After the Fall* (Verso, 1991). It is not about the Russian Revolution per se so much as a lengthy discussion on the possibilities and limitations of socialist planning and the market. I won't try to analyse Rees's discussion of the Blackburn piece here, because a different set of issues are involved.
3   J Rees, *International Socialism* 52, p5.
4   S Farber, op cit, p99.
5   Ibid, p109.
6   J Rees, op cit, p65.
7   Ibid, pp18ff.
8   Ibid, p22.
9   S Farber, op cit, pp57-59.
10   J Rees, op cit, p29.
11   Ibid, pp29-30.
12   R Tucker, *From Lenin to Gorbachev* (Norton, 1987), p84.
13   J Rees, op cit, p30.
14   Ibid, p70.
15   This choice, in itself revealing, is apparently the SWP's party line, since a review of *Before Stalinism* was published in the SWP's monthly *Socialist Review* under the title 'The New Menshevism'. This review, by Phil Gasper, also appears in the September 1991 issue of the ISO paper under the title 'Did Leninism Lead to Stalinism?' Thus the 'New Menshevism' title is not Gasper's but the British SWP's own invention. It must be said that Gasper's method of quotation and argument is infinitely more honest than that of Rees's article. Gasper nonetheless misses Sam's point in at least two key respects: (a) He writes that Farber 'seems to believe that after 1921 the eventual triumph of Stalinism was inevitable.' This is *not* Sam's view; indeed it is closer to what is implied by Rees. (b) He writes that, 'The fundamental weakness in Farber's book is his failure to grasp' that 'Stalinism represented not a continuation of the politics of Lenin and the Bolsheviks, but a counter-revolution.' Really! This kind of thing can be laughed off as good natured sectarian foolery, but Gasper should be reminded that some of his readers may be naive enough to take it seriously.

A reply to John Rees

ROBIN BLACKBURN

John Rees's article 'In Defence of October' (*International Socialism*, 52) advances a justification of the leaders of the Russian Revolution of 1917-21 and claims to rebut recent socialist writings which try to draw up a critical balance sheet of Bolshevism. The contingent justification of the Bolsheviks is rather well done—but the same cannot be said of the riposte to Farber, Hobsbawm, Slovo and myself. This having been said, I must confess I felt absolutely no discomfort reading the article at all. Rees could have made clearer the evident differences between those he is criticising, but I did not feel unhappy, either at being included in their number, or at the occasional selective references to my article. I quickly gathered that the author had a single minded determination to defend the Bolshevik record and that the references to myself and others were a sort of polemical garnish. Writing a piece like this is a considerable undertaking and maybe the author's adversarial zeal helped him to carry it out. Facile critics of Bolshevism should be abashed by the material it contains but not most of the left writers that Rees targeted. Perhaps an author's primary duty is to his own argument, not to doing justice to everybody else's—though it is always impressive when both tasks are combined.

I think some comments are in order just in case readers of *International Socialism* imagine that Rees really did deal with the arguments of Farber, Hobsbawm or myself. The interest of these criticisms of Bolshevism surely arises from the fact that they come from people who, by background and conviction, are scarcely sworn enemies of October. Indeed it may be that most of us still see more in the Russian Revolution to defend than does Rees himself. I would certainly be disposed to credit the Russian Revolution, and the state it established, with playing a critical role in the eventual military defeat of Nazism, with a generally positive contribution to anti-colonial and anti-imperialist struggles, and with providing somewhat more favourable conditions for the Western workers' struggles for better rights and conditions. I am referring here to the broad objective impact of the revolution, and the state it established, not to the particular policies of Soviet rulers who often sought to accommodate themselves to capitalist forces. Strangely enough, John Rees, in his lengthy article, does not deal with such matters which surely have some bearing on the ultimate historical significance of the Russian Revolution.

Rees's defence of October seems to imply two different arguments. Firstly, there is the line of defence which treats the Russian Revolution as a somewhat more sustained Paris Commune, a heroic defeat displaying at once the creativity of popular or proletarian revolution and the barbarism of reaction. On such a view the 'force of circumstance' and stark historical conditions put into the shade the mistake of the revolutionary leaders. I do not think that Slovo, Hobsbawm or Farber would deny that there was an historical grandeur to the Russian Revolution and that Lenin had a far firmer grasp of its political dynamic than the majority of his political opponents.

But Rees seems to be straining for another conclusion, namely that revolutions of essentially the Russian type still offer us a model. For a variety of reasons this is a conclusion that I would strongly contest. The Russian Revolution took place in a society where bourgeois institutions of all types were weak and bourgeois representative democracy a very frail import. I think Rees's own account of the lack of popular esteem for the Constituent Assembly may have a relevance he has not noticed. There are today few countries where bourgeois democratic assemblies are as little esteemed as was the case in Russia in 1917-18. The existence of the soviets meant that the Constituent Assembly did not have the sort of monopoly on general political representation which is the norm for such representative bodies today. Indeed the experience of 'dual power' must now seem to be rather exceptional in the light of the history of the 20th century. In Russian conditions the backdrop of a crumbling feudal Absolutist order combined with an exceptionally weak bourgeoisie allowed a new anti-bourgeois power to consolidate itself and to bypass the Constituent Assembly, though even in Russia the Bolsheviks themselves paid some tribute to the legitimacy of the Assembly by calling for it to be elected and convened. And they soon discovered the enduring significance of bourgeois representative assemblies in much of the rest of Europe.

Lenin in *Left Wing Communism* and Trotsky in his writings on Germany both memorably warned of the dangers of underestimating bourgeois democracy or failing to establish a vigorous revolutionary presence within it. No doubt Lenin and Trotsky were still inclined at this time to go on regarding the Russian Revolution as a model. But we now have the perspective of a further half century. Fascism waş overthrown in Germany and Italy in the 1940s, and in Spain and Portugal in the 1970s, without workers' councils bidding to become rival state structures. Colonialism has been thrown back nearly everywhere without workers' councils playing the key role. Stalinism has been overthrown in Eastern Europe and the Soviet Union without the appearance of institutions of dual power. Hungary had workers' councils in 1956 and Poland had Solidarity in 1980. But if representative assemblies had been conceded would they have been rejected by the Hungarian or Polish working class? I doubt it. France in 1968 and Portugal in 1974-5 did not throw up workers' councils either—in both cases the revolutionary movement was outflanked by the holding of elections to a bourgeois democratic assembly. Saudi Arabia is the only political entity which today might be compared with Tsarist Russia. Perhaps we will see workers' councils there—I certainly hope so—but without depreciating the Saudi revolution I do not think that the rest of the world will follow the same pattern. Where consent of the governed has been solicited by democratic representative bodies I do not think it is either practical or desirable for socialists to imagine that they can be ignored or bypassed. Typically such institutions will be hedged around with a host of undemocratic features and these should be campaigned against by socialists. And situations may arise in which one set of democratic institutions are arrayed against another, weaker and less democratic set, in which case a different sort of dual power will appear. Thus a Scottish Assembly might find itself at loggerheads with Westminster and British socialists might decide to support it. But that would be a quite different scenario to 1917. I would imagine that this is what Hobsbawm was driving at when he refers to the Russian Revolution as a 'freak result'.

None of the authors directly criticised by Rees, so far as I am aware, makes very much of the dispersal of the Constituent Assembly. Samuel Farber, who offers by far the most detailed account, stresses that he believes this particular Bolshevik decision to have been justified. What he criticises is the many ways in which the Bolsheviks violated the democratic workings of the soviets—overturning of elections, non-convening of meetings, intimidation of minority currents and so forth. I think his account is a sobering one, raising many serious questions, even if, as I said in my article, I think he does not give sufficient weight to the terrible constraints of the times—both the conduct of the Whites, the ravages of famine and the bloody example given by the supposedly advanced countries in their own Great War. But while I agree that Farber does not take due account of the force of circumstances I think his book is very valuable because it makes it clear what a flawed model this really is and because it draws attention to the existence of currents *within Bolshevism* which contested this or that unfortunate or deplorable decision.

While Farber gives insufficient weight to the 'force of circumstance' argument, he does arouse the lively suspicion that many arbitrary measures were adopted as harsh necessities when they were not actually necessities at all; and, once adopted, there was a tendency to glorify them, so that they became, officially, not harsh necessities at all but expressions of revolutionary virtue and a party minded spirit. In this category could come the celebration of the absence of law as a positive feature of the workers' state, the introduction of one man management in most branches of industry, the wholesale forced requisition of foodstuffs from the peasantry, the falsification of elections to the soviets, the failure to convene the Central Executive of the Soviets, the harassment of even those anarchists and Mensheviks who favoured active collaboration with the Reds, the application of the death penalty, contrary to soviet legislation, to suspects arrested outside the war zone and much else all copiously documented by Farber. Of course by the standards of Ypres and the Somme, or of European colonial warfare, the Bolsheviks could be regarded as quite restrained and humanitarian. But that does not mean that all their arbitrary measures were indeed harsh necessities since, as Farber shows, they were often counter-productive even in terms of beating the Whites and corresponded instead to a sort of Jacobin frenzy, as Rosa Luxemburg noted.

John Rees is shocked at my contention that Lenin was 'not a systematic thinker'. This quote was extracted from a sentence which paid tribute to an aspect of Lenin's thought: 'Lenin, though not a systematic thinker, actually developed a greater grasp than Marx of the necessary complexity of both politics and economics.' What I had in mind here was that Lenin's writings on the party, on the limits of trade union consciousness or on parliamentarism addressed questions which Marx never really considered. On the other hand Lenin did not reconcile what he had said about the party in his earlier writings with what he wrote about soviets in *State and Revolution*. The practice of a party dictatorship corresponded, perhaps, to a certain silence in these texts. While Lenin practised pluralism within the workers' movement he did not theorise it. It was possible to conclude from his writings that ideally there should only be one party, that representing the true interests of workers, in the workers' state. Does John Rees himself subscribe to this view? Indeed I would be interested to know whether the editors of *International Socialism* think that there is a necessary role for law in a socialist democracy. Do they think that workers should have more votes than members of the middle classes, or the retired, or housewives? It may be that I am wrong in supposing that we will not see workers' committees challenge the sovereignty of parliament. I think those who believe this owe us some sort of account of the political principles which would inform these new institutions of a workers' democracy. For my own part I am sure that bourgeois democracy can be greatly improved upon—but not by regressing to assemblies without party competition, or without legal defence of the right to disagree, or without universal and equal adult suffrage. The reader of Rees's critique might suppose that my argument had been comprehensively dealt with.[1] Actually the principal theme of my piece—the need for a workable picture of a socialist economy—was not even mentioned. The Bolsheviks were forced into 'War Communism' by what they saw as military necessity. In the 1919 party programme they committed themselves to intoxicating visions of the suppression of commodity relations. Among other things I try to show that Trotsky came to reject the view that the outright suppression of market relations was either necessary or desirable. His November 1932 essay on 'The Dangers Facing the Soviet Economy' published in the *Bulletin of the Opposition* contained a remarkable analysis showing that the power of the ruling bureaucracy was itself based on a voluntaristic attempt to suppress market relations. This might achieve limited goals but would breed great economic irrationality and would be contrary to the interests of the direct producers. While I can well imagine that the editors of *International Socialism* will not agree with the conclusions I advance in this essay I do think they should explain their own view of the sort of economic institutions that would characterise a genuinely socialist economic system. I suppose they would support a system embodying public ownership, planning and workers' control. But would they subscribe to the vision of workers' self management developed by Ernest Mandel in *New Left Review*, 159, or Diane Elson in *NLR*, 171, or Pat Devine in his book, *Democracy and Economic Planning*? It is all very well saying that workers' committees are to run everything, but how are prices to be arrived at? What happens when one committee disagrees with another? What assurance is there that 'socially necessary labour' really is socially necessary? Presumably means will have to be found for making producers' views on this question harmonious with the views of consumers (communities as well as individuals). And since socialism can only really exist on a global basis, to what extent would a worldwide planning authority actually control production? How would it tackle the appalling problems of poverty, inequality and ecological danger bequeathed by capitalism, yet not attempt the impossible and undesirable task of prescribing how much of everything is produced, and for whom?

These are the sort of questions which it is now even more necessary than before for socialists to answer, or at least debate. However much we may admire the heroism and creativity of Russian workers in 1917 the revolution itself was eventually lost—and the revolution itself usurped. Those of us who advocate the suppression of capitalism will be expected to explain why we expect things to turn out quite differently next time. And that cannot be done by dwelling only on the heroic aspects of October, and neglecting to consider the ways in which Bolshevism may itself have provided openings for the rise of Stalinism.

Notes

1   My essay is reprinted in Robin Blackburn (ed), *After the Fall: the Failure of Communism and the Future of Socialism* (Verso, 1991). While Rees finds me too critical of Lenin, Neal Ascherson, reviewing this book for the *London Review of Books*, 6 March 1992, chides me with being too indulgent towards Lenin and the Bolsheviks. This divergent criticism leads me to believe that I've got it about right. Incidentally I do try to make clear in this somewhat expanded version of my essay that Luxemburg was not wholly in the right in her criticism of the Bolsheviks, though I believe her vindication of pluralism remains fundamental.

Dedicated followers of fashion

JOHN REES

The history of great revolutions is always refracted through the prism of contemporary politics. The English Revolution has long had its hostile narrators on the right and, on the left, its fate has been fought over by Whig and Marxist historians. The relative popularity of these interpretations has been largely shaped by the contours of the domestic class struggle. But the influence of conflicting interpretations of the Russian Revolution has been decided by international considerations: on the one hand the success of popular movements from below, and on the other hand the rivalry between the various imperial powers. Understanding this context is as vital to understanding the revolution as a grasp of the relevant historical facts.

'In Defence of October' was written, not for the quasi-psychological motives attributed to me by Robin Blackburn, but because there is a marked shift in this debate for the first time since the 1960s. The Cold War produced its own viciously anti-socialist orthodoxy and a corresponding attitude to the October revolution—Lenin led to Stalin. The Stalinists had their own reasons for endorsing this view. In the 1960s and 1970s this orthodoxy was challenged, not just by Trotskyists and other anti-Stalinist socialists, but by a number of academics influenced both by social upheaval in the West and by the moves towards detente between the superpowers.

The East European revolutions and the subsequent collapse of the USSR have inevitably reshaped the intellectual landscape once more. The Stalinist model has been demolished—but the right wing, in the historiography of the revolution as in reality, have so far been the major beneficiaries. One reason for this is that many on the left shared some or all of the assumptions about the nature of Russian society which underpinned the Stalinist model and therefore found themselves ideologically disarmed in the face of a newly confident right wing.

Robert Service simply denies that very many 'scholars or commentators nowadays contend that there was an inevitability about the passage...from Lenin to the Stalinist programme of the 1930s'. Two points need to be made about this assertion: i) 'In Defence of October' produced a significant amount of evidence, notably from Stephen Cohen and Edward Acton, to the contrary[1] and ii) Robert Service's own article is testimony that this argument is alive and well.

'Did Lenin Lead to Stalin?' shrinks from using the word 'inevitable', settling instead for the claim that 'only the wilfully blind would fail to see that those continuities are very strong indeed.' The construction of the Stalinist regime is, in Robert Service's account, a single, continuous and unbroken process. The one party state was:

in a condition of partial construction before the October revolution. The scaffolding for its walls was in place by the middle of the civil war. The roof was added at the inception of the New Economic Policy...

Rarely has the 'malignant straight line' theory (Stephen Cohen's phrase quoted in my original article),[2] received such a concise formulation. Lenin's Bolshevism 'contained many genes which were to produce Stalinism'. Thus, 'even if not Stalin but Trotsky or Bukharin or even Kamenev had assumed the supreme party leadership after Lenin's death, an ultra-authoritarian system of rule would have prevailed.'

But perhaps this is because the desperate straits in which the revolution found itself would have imposed similar policies on anyone who led it? Nothing so historical. The real problem, according to Robert Service, is that 'there really was something violent and authoritarian both about Bolshevism from its inception after the turn of the century and about the October revolution...' So Trotsky merely argued for a 'milder variant of Bolshevism than Stalin's. But it was still Bolshevism'. This is the theory of original sin: Lenin ate of the apple in 1903 and damnation followed in 1917.

Mere historical facts are of little use in combating this kind of reasoning: the judgment has already been made. Nevertheless, it is worth correcting some of the inaccuracies with which 'Did Lenin lead to Stalin?' tries to bolster its metaphysics. Lenin, we are told, did not try to 'terminate' Stalin's political career because he did not recommend his expulsion from the party. Yet surely the removal of

Stalin as general secretary was designed to remove him from all effective power. Lenin had rarely recommended anything more severe. Zinoviev and Kamenev, whom Lenin described as scabs and strikebreakers for their role in publicly opposing the October revolution, were two of the few prominent Bolsheviks who would have suffered expulsion from the party if Lenin had had his way. But Lenin did not get his way. Indeed, far from being 'bossy' and 'obsessive', Lenin continued to work with Zinoviev and Kamenev, as he continued to work with Bukharin during and after Bukharin led the opposition to the Brest-Litovsk treaty which almost resulted in a split in the Bolsheviks.

Lenin's tolerance for such debate, right up to and including the 10th party congress, belies the tale that he shared Stalin's desire for a 'single unchallengeable ideology'. Similarly, the contention that both Lenin and Stalin deployed 'terror whenever the party's power was thought to be threatened' obscures much more than it reveals. Lenin did advocate the use of force, predominantly against those who used force, or gave succour to those who used force, against the revolution.

Robert Service's own example of the treatment of Russian Orthodox bishops in 1922 is a case in point. This seemingly despotic act was actually committed in the midst of famine in which a total of 5 million died; the bishops were hoarding gold that could have paid to help feed the starving. The law was carefully framed so that removal of valuables would only take place in the presence of believers and so that no object would be removed that was necessary for worship. Here is a rather less distorted account of events following the proclamation of a law sequestrating church valuables for the aid of famine victims:

Patriarch Tikhon...branded this law as sacrilegious and non-canonical, and called upon the faithful to resist its realisation with every available means. The agitation which began was carried on in much the same way as the previous agitation against the 1918 decree separating church and state, but with the difference that the issue was now of an entirely humanitarian nature...

To argue the question on the basis of church canons and state laws in a country just emerging from a state of war and revolution and struggling for the very life of starving millions was a futile task. Even legally, religious groups could not refuse to return to the state that which they had received for use only and for which they had signed contracts to that effect...

The conflict that developed between the church and the government, because of the Patriarch's resistance, claimed not a few victims. There were riots with some bloodshed, followed by repressive measures on the part of the state...In all were reported 45 executions and 250 long term imprisonments. The church throughout the country was in a state of anarchy. Large sections of it, particularly in the famine area, resented the Patriarch's stand...[3]

Indeed, when the house arrest of the Patriarch became known, Bishop Antonine and priests Vedensky, Belkoff and Krasnitsky led a group to the Patriarch's residence:

the day before the execution of the Moscow priests, they appeared before the Patriarch and remonstrated with him that he was chiefly responsible for the terror and the anarchy in the church and that with his name was associated the whole counter revolutionary policy of the church in recent years. They forced the retirement of the Patriarch and appealed to the church to make peace with the new social order.[4]

But Robert Service is right about one thing concerning Lenin's attitude to the clergy at this time: 'his plan derived not from some definite anti-regime plot'. No it was the far more important consideration of saving at least some of the millions who were losing their lives. In the end, 'the amount of surplus wealth taken from the church was enormous, and yet so much remains that its loss is hardly noticeable to the visitor'.[5] Naturally one expects that a Professor of History and the School of Slavonic and East European Studies would at least mention this historical context.

Stalin's terror, on the contrary, was not used to alleviate famine. Nor did it defend the revolution or Lenin's Bolshevik Party—it destroyed both. Stalin's terror tried to eliminate great swathes of the population and succeeded in eliminating virtually the entire leadership and many of the rank and file of Lenin's Bolsheviks. Such an internal civil war was necessary precisely because the transition from Lenin's regime to Stalin's state was not simply a quantitative change, as Robert Service contends, but a difference in kind, the difference between a workers' revolution, albeit degenerated, and the emergence of a new ruling class.

Sam Farber and David Finkel, the attorney who deals with the legalistic side of Sam Farber's affairs, object to being associated with the kind of establishment historical opinion which Robert Service's article represents. They argue that *Before Stalinism* was misrepresented and should have been interpreted as a useful addition to the revolutionary argument. David Finkel barely bothers to address the substantive issues, mostly confining himself to his brief. He is wrong on all points and readers who are interested to know why will find my reply in the footnotes.[6]

Sam Farber does raise some issues of importance. The first concerns the trade unions. He baulks at using the kind of language that Robert Service employs (the party 'thrust its jackboot into the face of the labour movement'), but his argument bears a strong family likeness. The Bolsheviks were anti-union from as early as 1917, claims Sam Farber, quoting Zinoviev's argument that trade unions are unnecessary in a workers' state and noting his 'explicit rejection of the right to strike'.

Typically he does not quote Lenin's 1921 rebuttal of this same argument when it was advanced by Trotsky:

> *Trotsky seems to say that in a workers' state it is not the business of the trade unions to stand up for the material and spiritual interest of the working class. That is a mistake. Comrade Trotsky speaks of a 'workers' state'. May I say that this is an abstraction...it is...a patent error to say: 'Since this is a workers' state without any bourgeoisie, against whom then is the working class to be protected, and for what purposes?' Ours is a workers' state* **with a bureaucratic twist to it**.
>
> *We now have a state under which it is the business of the massively organised proletariat to protect itself, while we must use the workers' organisation to protect the workers from their state, and get them to protect our state.*[7]

But perhaps Sam Farber doesn't quote Lenin because he believes this statement to be 'no more than symbolic'? So whose ideas were reflected in the practice of the trade unions, Zinoviev's or Lenin's? Sam seems to have forgotten the answer he himself gave in *Before Stalinism*. There he noted that though there was disillusionment with the unions in the mid-1920s:

> *Yet, strikes had not been outlawed. Thus, and even though the unions pursued a no-strike policy, there were reports of 102 strikes involving 43,000 workers in 1921-22, and 267 strikes involving 42,000 workers...in 1924. In 1925 no strikes were sanctioned by the unions but there were still 186 strikes involving 43,000 workers. In 1926 there were 327 strikes involving 32,900 strikers in state industries...*[8]

None of this is to deny the very real degeneration of the revolution that was taking place during this period or that such degeneration affected the trade unions. Nevertheless, even when there were formal restrictions on union democracy it would be wrong to conclude that democratic debate on trade union issues did not take place in the key institutions of the revolution. Arthur Ransome, for instance, records the 1920 debate on trade union issues at a conference at Jaroslavl held in preparation for the All-Russian Communist conference. The old Menshevik Larin opposes one man management in industry. After a heated debate:

> *Larin and Radek severally summed up and made final attacks on each others' positions, after which Radek's resolution approving the theses of the Central Committee was passed almost unanimously. Larin's four amendments received one, three, seven and one vote apiece. This result was received with cheering throughout the theatre, and showed the importance of such conferences in smoothing the way of the dictatorship, since it had been obvious when the discussion began that a very much larger proportion of the delegates than finally voted for his resolution had been in sympathy with Larin in his opposition to the Central Committee.[9]*

After the vote delegates were elected to the All-Russian conference. Larin declined to stand but:

> *Rostopchin put it to the conference that although they disagreed with Larin, yet it would be as well that he should have the opportunity of stating his views at the All-Russian conference, so that the discussion should be as many-sided as possible. The conference expressed its agreement with this. Larin withdrew his withdrawal, and was presently elected.[10]*

Of course discussions like this are not the same as discussions inside the trade unions themselves and Sam Farber is quite right to point to the spread of the practice of appointing union and party officials by the mid-1920s. But he is hardly original in making this point. Indeed the 'mainstream Bolshevik tradition', which he is so keen to denigrate, made precisely these points. Trotsky's first attack on the bureaucracy, partly in response to a wave of strikes in Sormovo, Kharkov and the Donets Basin, insisted that:

> *the present regime...is much farther from workers' democracy than the regime of the fiercest period of War Communism. The bureaucratisation of the party apparatus has developed to unheard of proportions by means of the method of secretarial selection...dissatisfaction...does not dissipate itself by way of influence of the mass upon the party organisation (election of party committees, secretaries, etc) but accumulates in secret and thus leads to interior strains...[11]*

Socialist legality is the second issue which Sam Farber raises. Again he will not quite use Robert Service's phraseology (legal nihilists), merely insisting that Lenin saw 'lawlessness as an intrinsic feature of the "dictatorship of the proletariat".'

So were Lenin and the Bolsheviks monsters with no care for the justice or otherwise of individual cases, simply arresting and executing people because of their class origin? 'In Defence of October' showed that Lenin completely rejected this idea when it was advanced by

Latsis, one of the leaders of the Cheka, and cited a series of incidents where Lenin personally intervened to correct injustices.[12] To this we can add instances recorded in John Keep's recent and largely hostile account of the early months of Bolshevik rule.[13] The first incident involved the murder of two leading Cadets by anarchist sailors. Keep tells us Lenin took this seriously, 'bombarding the investigators with requests for information (nine actions from 7 to 31 January)'—but that in the end the case fizzled out since the perpetrators could not be found.[14] In a second incident Lenin backed strenuous investigation into accusations of arbitrary searches and profiteering by Red Guards, although he was by no means convinced of their guilt.[15]

But what of the wider question, raised both by Sam Farber and Robin Blackburn: do revolutionaries stand for the systematic and equal application of the law? It would be easy to give the glib answer—that any democrat, let alone socialist, wants to see justice done and that this involves people knowing what the law is and only being prosecuted for demonstrably breaking it. That is certainly what we would wish to be the case in a socialist society. But such a situation can only exist where there is a social consensus to the effect that the law makers and the system of justice are legitimate. In capitalist society most of the time the ruling order, through a mixture of force, fraud and propaganda, can convince a large enough section of the population of their legitimacy to enable the 'rule of law' to prevail. A revolution and civil war are, by definition, times when no such consensus, and therefore no such legitimacy, exists.

The case of the bishops who hoarded church riches, cited above, is an example. Despite their explicit recognition of the separation of church and state, despite signing legal documents that the church riches now belonged to state agreed trustees and despite the Patriarch's public guarantee not to enter the political arena, the church took the first available opportunity to break all such undertakings. And it did not break them in a way which would allow simple police methods of arrest and trial to deal with the question. It chose methods of class warfare—calling on its followers to use any available means to resist the government.

Faced with such situations, and the revolution and civil war were replete with far more dangerous examples than this, the Bolsheviks moved between trying to establish a socialist legal framework and themselves having to use the methods of open warfare. And in warfare individual justice (did this particular soldier point his rifle at me and am I therefore justified in shooting at him in reply?) is inevitably replaced by categorical judgments (is he or she on our side or not?)[16]. One wishes for the former, but cannot rule out the latter. It is for precisely this reason that I recorded the judgement of such a hostile witness as George Leggett in my original analysis:

> *in the inevitable clash between the arbitrary violence of the Cheka and the system of Soviet law evolved by the People's Commissariat for Justice, the Cheka gained the upper hand whenever the regime came under threat; when crises receded the [People's Commissariat] won the advantage.*[17]

Sam Farber objects to having his account of the revolution likened to those of the right wing. In one sense of course he is right: Sam's *intention* is to strengthen the socialist tradition, not to bury it. But he nevertheless uses arguments which are close relatives of those deployed by the right because he rejects 'mainstream Bolshevism' and because his analytical method is badly flawed.

Sam's rejection of 'mainstream Bolshevism' is conducted under the banner of a possible alternative outcome of events which he sees latent in the criticisms of Lenin advanced by the Right and Left Bolsheviks in the 1920s. The chapter in *Before Stalinism* entitled 'Alternatives to Lenin' has sections dealing with Right Bolsheviks, Left Bolsheviks, anarchists and Left Social Revolutionaries—but no section on the Left Opposition and only a handful of references to Trotsky. So when Sam claims that 'all my specific criticisms of "Leninism in power" were made *at the time* by...the early Left and Right Bolshevik oppositions' he is right. But he has chosen to construct a retrospective ahistorical alternative composed of a pick and mix of all their programmes. Now, of course, if there were an animal which was half sheep and half pig we could happily carve pork chops and lamb chops from the same carcass. The Left and Right Bolsheviks had mutually incompatible programmes in every area—foreign policy, the peasantry, the economy, military affairs—which is why an effective opposition could not emerge until Trotsky built an opposition based on an economic and social, as well as democratic, alternative to the bureaucracy.

But *Before Stalinism*'s search for an alternative to mainstream Bolshevism is not really to do with the history of 1920s Russia. It is to do with political organisation in the 1990s. Sam Farber rejects Lenin's model of the party as 'Jacobin'—and since this conception of the party was with Lenin since at least 1902, and since Sam Farber clearly believes it was an important cause of the degeneration of the revolution, it is pointless, though understandable, for him to deny that his thesis bolsters the right wing's claim that 'the authoritarian character of "Leninism in power" was already built into the original conceptions of Bolshevism'.

The charge of Jacobinism is itself misguided. The authoritarian nature of the societies established by bourgeois revolutions does not, in any case, stem primarily from the political forms of organisation adopted by the revolutionaries. Rather both are a function of the fact that the bourgeoisie is itself a minority, albeit leading a majority against the old order, and therefore tends to develop such organisations as can mobilise the masses but at the same time represent the bourgeoisie's own sectional interest against the masses.

The need for a revolutionary party springs from the quite different profile of the workers' revolution. Here the problem is that although the revolution represents 'a movement of the immense majority, in the interests of the immense majority', the process by which a class moves into struggle and becomes politically conscious is both uneven and lengthy. If the minority of revolutionaries created by day to day struggles are to survive and to have influence on the subsequent course of the struggle they must necessarily organise themselves, even though they are for the time being a minority. How this minority becomes the majority involves the whole body of revolutionary strategy and tactics. Clearly there are dangers, both that the minority will become impatient and substitute itself for the class and that it will become demoralised and dissolve itself or blunt its revolutionary politics. But this problem cannot be wished away with talk of Jacobinism.

Such political positions carry a methodological dimension. Sam has accomplished the astounding feat of writing an entire book about the rise of Stalinism without ever saying exactly what sort of society he believes Russia had become by the 1930s. Was it a new class society, state capitalist or what? The answer to this question matters because if you see the rise of Stalinism involving a social counter-revolution then the economic and international isolation of the regime became crucial because it deprived the Bolsheviks of the material basis for socialism. If, however, this is not the case it opens the way to locate the transition to socialism only, or mainly, at the political level. This seems to be Sam Farber's position as his quotation of Rakovsky's point about income differentials and political influence being the defining characteristic of the bureaucracy indicates.[18] Further evidence for this interpretation comes from the way in which *Before Stalinism* locates the origin of such repressive societies as China, Cuba and Vietnam. These 'revolutionary leaderships', we are told, 'made conscious political choices favouring undemocratic political arrangements...not as lesser evils imposed by...economic and other objective difficulties'.[19]

All this, in turn, opens the way for an analysis of the October revolution which insists that democracy, legality and a socialist constitution could have turned the tide where Trotsky failed. Hence Sam's summary of his position:

the moment the working class is deprived of democratic control over the institutions through which it exercises power in society, that working class has lost its power, period.

There is no gainsaying this as a general statement, but it utterly fails as an account of the degeneration of the Russian Revolution. In this context it would be far more accurate to say that *the moment the working class ceases to exist as a social force even the most democratic institutions will lose their power over society.* The isolation of the revolution meant the destruction of the working class in the civil war and the famine that followed—which is why concentration on the purely political is not an antidote to determinism but a failure to observe the most elementary requirements of the Marxist method.

Since Robin Blackburn relies exclusively on Sam Farber for his interpretation of the October revolution, I hope that I have already supplied adequate replies to at least some of the issues raised in 'A Reply to John Rees'. He does however go on to raise a number of questions about the contemporary relevance of the October revolution which require a response.

Let me begin by giving answers to two direct questions posed by Robin Blackburn: does the tradition in which *International Socialism* stands believe in socialist legality and a plurality of parties and do we have any analysis of the kind of economic structure which a socialist society would entail? The first point is easily answered. Of course we believe in socialist legality and a plurality of parties—and so did the Bolsheviks until the darkest days of the civil war. But, as I have already said in my reply to Sam Farber, to win such freedoms requires victory in a class struggle. Only on that basis can the consensus necessary for the operation of any form of legality be established. And in that struggle the laws of battle will sometimes contradict the rules of polite debate. Our chances of success are greater than those faced by the Bolsheviks for the very good reason that we hope to be at the head of a working class that is the overwhelming majority of the population, not one which numbered merely 3 million out of total population of 160 million, and in an advanced industrialised country, not in a still largely peasant land.

The economic structure of a socialist society cannot be fully examined here. But Robin Blackburn is mistaken in believing that it has not been a subject of discussion in our tradition. The Bolsheviks' early attempts at a mixture of state guided and market mechanisms were referred to in 'In Defence of October'. Robin Blackburn himself has noted Trotsky's writings on the same subject. Related issues have been examined by Chris Harman in 'The Myth of the Market' (*International Socialism* 42), and Alex Callinicos who devoted a considerable part of his book, *The Revenge of History*, to the kind of political and economic structure that a socialist society might need.

But Robin Blackburn's major objection to 'In Defence of October' is that it argues that the Bolshevik experience still supplies us with a model for a socialist strategy today. This is mistaken, the argument runs, because the Bolsheviks failed to appreciate 'the enduring significance of bourgeois representative assemblies in much of the rest of Europe' and could only pursue a successful revolutionary strategy in Russia because 'bourgeois institutions of all types were weak and bourgeois representative democracy a very frail import'. Of the great revolutionary upheavals of the 20th century only Hungary in 1956 and Poland in 1980 have given rise to genuine institutions of workers' power and even these could have been dispersed easily enough if a bourgeois democratic set up had been granted.

One immediate result of Robin Blackburn's analysis is that the collapse of the distinctive features of class politics, whether of the reformist variety or of the revolutionary tradition, is taken to extremes. 'In Defence of October' noted that one result of the left wing attacks on the Bolshevik tradition was that 'much of what now passes for socialist thought is indistinguishable from run of the mill liberalism'. Sadly, Robin Blackburn has all too quickly provided a striking example.[20]

The historical 'facts' which supposedly underpin this shift are quite wrong. In the all important German Revolution of 1919-23 workers' councils were ranged against bourgeois parliaments. The decisive factor in the defeat of the revolution was the inexperience of the revolutionaries, not the legitimacy of the National Assembly. The Finnish revolution of 1918 failed for similar reasons, as did the Spanish revolution of 1936. In Chile in the early 1970s the inter-factory committees, the cordones, threatened to become an alternative centre of power for the working class to that of Allende's left wing government, and this in a country known as 'the Britain of Latin America' for its supposed stability. Similarly, whether the crises in France in 1968 and Portugal in the mid-1970s developed into revolutionary situations was not, in the final analysis, a question of loyalty to bourgeois institutions but of political leadership, although not simply in a narrow or immediate sense. A decisive factor in many of these cases was the influence of Stalinist popular front politics—strangely, the very politics Robin Blackburn is so keen to see revived in the form of Charter 88.

It should scarcely need saying that the legitimacy of bourgeois democracy even in the advanced capitalist states rests not on some timeless historical loyalty on the part of workers but largely on their ability to sustain the standard of living of the population. Yet this is a time when even American workers have lost 17 percent of their real income in a generation, when the core of the European economy,

Germany, is more unstable than it has been at any time in the post-war period, when the great series of recessions which opened in the early 1970s shows every sign of deepening and when the great bogey of the Stalinist states has vanished. As I write, Los Angeles is under a curfew enforced by tanks and over 10,000 troops, a fact reported in *The Observer* under the headline 'Superpower retakes gutted second city' and with the words 'the upsurge of anger in New York and a score of other cities showed how precarious the normal order is.'[21] It seems a poor time to be arguing, Fukuyama style, the historical inviolability of bourgeois democracy.

What connects all these responses is that they are written by people who have altered their appraisal of the October revolution under the twin impact of the fall of Stalinism and the collapse of the enthusiasm which was generated by the struggles of the late 1960s and early 1970s.[22] Then fashion dictated at least a sympathetic hearing for the Bolsheviks if not outright identification with revolutionary politics. Now intellectual fashion—for there have been only essentially minor revelations of new historical facts about the revolution[23]—dictate a different tune. Transitory notoriety can be attained by such methods but the socialist movement requires more constant companions.

Notes

1 'In Defence of October', *International Socialism* 52, pp10, 11 and 18.
2 Ibid, p18.
3 JF Hecker, *Religion and Communism* (London, 1933) pp207-20. I am grateful to Mike Haynes for this reference.
4 Ibid, pp209-210.
5 Ibid, p209.
6 David Finkel's contribution to this debate is remarkable if only for its tone. Why he should choose to write in this particularly abusive form is a mystery. Perhaps one reason is that he overestimates the degree to which 'In Defence of October' was directed at *Before Stalinism*. Eight references out of a total of 270 hardly constitutes a 'running polemic'. Nevertheless, let me deal with the points he raises:
    References 1 and 2: the first objection is that I accuse Sam Farber of believing that Lenin's pre civil war policies led to Stalin, the second that I deleted 'Farber's explicit specification of the period after the civil war as a focus of critical political analysis'. This point is particularly easy to deal with since David Finkel provides the refutation on the next but one page. Finkel reproduces, at slightly greater length but with no alteration in meaning (supposedly his second objection), the passage in which Sam Farber tells us that Lenin's distaste for codified rules 'had sometimes played an important role in his political practice concerning internal party organisation'. Finkel then adds: 'Examples are then cited from old factional battles between 1903 and 1909'. In other words, Lenin's pre-1917, never mind about pre-1921, policies *are* being used as evidence for his 'chronic distaste' for legal procedures. Finkel comments that 'obviously, this has *nothing* to do with the caricature...that the Bolsheviks were some kind of monolithic party'. Readers will have to judge for themselves how obvious this is.

Reference 3: This is a lengthy quote from 'In Defence of October' which even Finkel admits 'quotes without blatant distortion'. He then goes on to wonder about things that I 'imply', ie things that Finkel wishes I had said but which in fact I did not say.

Reference 4, concerns my supposedly ignoring the fact that Lenin and the Bolsheviks did not call the introduction of War Communism a retreat (as they did the introduction of the NEP). Yet 'In Defence of October' clearly quotes Lenin complaining that the nationalisation policies under War Communism were forced on them and that if they continued 'we shall inevitably be beaten' (p43). I also quote a Bolshevik leader of the Food Commissariat talking of food requisitioning, the other major social policy of War Communism, in these terms: 'What do you think, the People's Commissariat of Food Supply does this for its own satisfaction? No, we do it because there is not enough food' (p45). The forced, makeshift nature of War Communism is clear enough from contemporary statements, even without looking at Trotsky's and other Bolsheviks' later depositions on the accidental nature of developments in this period.

As to the use of the phrase 'Stalinist Leninism', I still maintain that no one keenly aware of the counter-revolutionary nature of Stalinism, of the river of blood running between the revolutionary tradition and the Stalinist tradition, should dream of employing such an expression.

Reference 4a and 4c: David Finkel clearly believes that when I quoted Farber on the White Terror my omission of the words 'in this context' was a 'cynical manipulation'. On the contrary, it does not alter my point at all; it is the omission of a full discussion of the White Terror which is a 'cynical manipulation' of the real history of the Russian civil war, and to do so in the name of isolating the 'political dimension' is to compound bad history with bad method. The same technique is used in the discussion of the Green Terror. Here the impact is even greater since knowledge of the brutality of the peasant risings is less widely known than that of the Whites.

Reference 4b: 'In Defence of October' claimed that Sam Farber quoted Latsis but did not quote Lenin. David Finkel's quotation from *Before Stalinism* shows that I was right—Farber mentions Lenin's objection in a phrase of two words and does not quote him. This lessens the impact of Lenin's forceful intervention and is typical of the way in which *Before Stalinism* uses a qualifying phrase to disguise the importance of the key episodes in the development of the Lenin government.

7   Quoted in T Cliff, *Trotsky Vol 2, The Sword of Revolution* (London, 1990) pp176-177.

8   S Farber, *Before Stalinism* (London, 1990) p88.

9   A Ransome, *The Crisis in Russia 1920* (London, 1992) pp52-53. This book and its companion volume, *Six Weeks in Russia 1919*, are reviewed by Sheila McGregor elsewhere in this journal.

10   Ibid, p53.

11   *Documents of the 1923 Opposition* (London, 1975) pp2-3.

12   'In Defence of October', op cit, p53 and p51.

13   J Keep, 'Lenin's Time Budget: the Smolny Period' in E R Frankel, J Frankel and B Knei-Paz (eds), *Revolution in Russia, reassessments of 1917* (London, 1992).

14   Ibid, p348.

15   Ibid, pp350-351.

16   Warfare is a suitable analogy, although the dangers of mistaking your enemy in a class war are obviously greater than in a conventional military struggle. Farber's analogy with the workers' bomb argument is, however, potty. We can say with a high degree of certainty that an exchange of nuclear weapons would destroy the working class, and that the use of categorical punishment, however undesirable recourse to such action might be, would not.

17 'In Defence of October', op cit, p54. Although Leggett is exaggerating in describing all Cheka operations as arbitrary violence.
18 *Before Stalinism*, op cit, p5.
19 Ibid, p3.
20 Although I did not dream that within a year Robin Blackburn would have carried that process so far as to call on socialists to vote Liberal in those constituencies where Labour was not best placed to beat the Tories in the British general election of 1992—advice which, if followed, would allow the Liberals to erode Labour support in exactly the way that the Labour Party built itself at the expense of the Liberals in the early decades of the century.
21 *The Observer*, 3 May 1992.
22 This is even true of Robert Service, whose best book, *The Bolshevik Party in Revolution* (London, 1979), was contemptuous of 'Robert Daniels, Leonard Shapiro and Merle Fainsod' who 'portray Bolshevik ideology as the original sin and regard Lenin as the greatest sinner' (p6).
23 One of the few exceptions is M Reiman's *The Birth of Stalinism* which, basing itself on German archives, shows that the Trotskyist opposition was stronger than previously thought and just how complete the break between Stalinism and the revolutionary tradition had to be.

In praise of custom

*A review of E P Thompson, **Customs in Common** (Merlin, 1991) £25*

COLIN BARKER

> *In our office, it's the custom that on your birthday you bring in a cake and put it in the kitchen, and everyone has some. The other day, it was the **manager's** birthday, and he brought a cake in. We had a meeting, and voted that we would not eat **his** cake. It sat in the kitchen all day. Oh, and it was such a beautiful chocolate cake....*

NALGO member, Manchester, 1991

Edward Thompson is one of the century's great historians. A new book by him is a significant event. This book is a collection of long essays, focused on 18th century England. Most have been previously published in journals. All are in one way or another concerned with 'popular custom'. They are characteristic of much of Thompson's work, as they strive to grasp the intimate textures of everyday life and simultaneously to reveal its 'political' character.

The subject matter is the class struggle. In other hands the issues explored here might be examples simply of antiquarianism. Why bother with 'rough music', wife-sales in public markets, changes in employers' and workers' sense of time, food riots and the like—other than to record what quaint and sometimes barbarous customs people used to have? But Thompson reveals in these issues something quite beyond the antiquarian's ken. He uncovers the struggles of ordinary people to control the circumstances of their own lives. In his pages representatives of the exploited and oppressed, working people in town and country, engage in ongoing struggles with their rulers. They fight over the very direction and meaning of social, economic and political life. These essays are chapters in those struggles.

Thompson writes beautifully. I'd read some of these essays before, and in preparing this review I've read the whole 538 pages twice over—they still give pleasure. His writing has a constant polemical edge, a pamphleteering quality and argumentative wit. A reviewer with a more 'professional' knowledge of social history might discuss this book differently, perhaps engaging with the author more directly on his own specialist ground. But I have not burrowed in old newspaper and pamphlet archives, nor even read very widely in the writings of those who have, and whose works are footnoted so extensively by Thompson. I come to this book as the fascinated reader, who knows little more about an activity like public wife-selling than the author tells me.

There are two interrelated themes in Thompson's essays. One is 'custom' as a central issue in the 18th century class struggle; the other, also drawing on 18th century materials, is 'custom' as a mechanism of community regulation.

Thompson rightly insists that to understand popular movements and 'popular culture' generally we need a proper sense of the whole context in which these develop. In a terrific opening chapter, 'The Patricians and the Plebs', he interrogates, gives a critique of and undermines the bland conservative account of 18th century England as a 'one-class society', where the gentry exercised a wise and kind 'paternal' government, and where apparently there was no class struggle. The whole picture, he shows, is a nonsense: this was a society ruled by a gang of wealthy and predatory parasites, reminiscent of a Latin American junta, and fawned on by client 'middle classes'[1]

That ruling class presided over a society undergoing a slow but inexorable transition towards the dominance of capitalism. Here 'paternalist' control over labour was slowly eroding. Workers were gaining more social independence from their 'masters' even as their economic dependence increased. The working people of 18th century England maintained an insubordination, self assertiveness and indiscipline that was the constant preoccupation of their 'betters'.

Yet until late in the 18th century—when the dual impulses of the American and French Revolutions were absorbed into popular ideas—ruling class 'hegemony' was fairly secure. When the rulers dealt with the poor and those they exploited they did so mostly through intermediaries; when they did appear in public, it was with 'much of the studied self-consciousness of public theatre'.[2] But at the same time, their 'hegemony' was anything but complete and direct. There were two cultural worlds, one patrician and the other plebeian, with not that many bridges connecting the two. *Their* Church of England no longer spoke to or connected with the social occasions, the feasts, festivals and rituals of the people. In circumstances where the classes lived in growing cultural alienation from each other, there existed a crucial space for 'popular custom' to flower without the direct involvement or supervision of the rulers' agencies. In the 19th century a more sober and utilitarian (and more worried) bourgeoisie would employ police measures to shut down and domesticate, 'license' and 'permit', 'police' and 'educate' the realm of popular culture and institutions. But in the 18th the rulers learned to live with, make concessions to and even flatter popular culture.

We have here a working class in the early phases of its own formation, developing forms of consciousness that were often anything but simply deferential: 'The mob may not have been noted for an impeccable consciousness of class; but the rulers of England were in no doubt at all that it was a horizontal sort of beast'.[3] Forms of popular struggle and self assertion were conditioned by the whole nexus of social relations in which the poor found themselves. The labourer might touch his forelock by day to farmer or squire; his masters knew him personally, and could hurt him seriously if he offended them. By night that same labourer might resort to bloodcurdling anonymous threats and acts of personal vengeance against their property. And that horizontal sort of beast, the crowd, could both be swift and direct in its action, and reveal a keen sense of how to ridicule and to negotiate with authority. If ruling class power in the courts and elsewhere was exercised with theatrical show, so was counter-power: in Harwich in 1724 the town's dignitaries were toasting His Hanoverian Majesty George's health, when a crowd of 200 carrying a fisherman dressed up with horns came 'drumming a ridiculous tune of Roundheaded Cuckolds &c, and (the fisherman) came to the Mayor's and this Deponent's door and made signs with his hands intimating that We might kiss his Arse'.[4]

Popular custom flourished in 18th century England 'defensively, in opposition to the constraints and controls of the patrician rulers'. It often appears conservative, because it was defensive—just as, later, trade unionism too has a conservative hue. What seems radical and innovative in the 18th century is an invading capitalist process, which takes form more concretely as sharpened exploitation, expropriation of customary use-rights, violent disruption of valued patterns of work and leisure. Popular custom had much to defend and conserve against this onslaught.

This was a world simultaneously under pressure from the expanding demands of capitalist rules and routines and yet also still living with inherited customary expectations and roles. Capitalism's advance threatened not just popular living standards in some simple material sense, but a whole way of life. 'Custom' was both a battlefield but also an arsenal of means of war. 'The common people' (GDH Cole's phrase) employed a variety of 'rituals' to enforce their own values and expectations both on their own members and against the local ruling class and its agents, the squire, the gamekeeper, the excise officer, or indeed the scab. Custom was a 'field of change and contest, an arena in which opposing interests made conflicting claims'.[5] Custom, then, was often the ordinary name of the class struggle. What's 'custom'? It has something of the meaning of 'culture', that 20th century 'clumpish term', but also something of the meaning of 'common law', of habitual usages, rules, obligations and rights. The 'conservatism' of popular custom was complex: the active process of defending a valued pattern of life also involved a deeply rebellious, anti-capitalist and anti-authoritarian side, and custom was regarded with polite suspicion and dislike.

A solid majority of Thompson's book is concerned with three areas of battle over custom, all of them centred on the opposition between capitalist requirements and customary assumptions. The first is landed property, the second is the price of food, and the third is time.

The 18th century witnessed one of the greatest waves of 'enclosure' of land. In various ways, that land had previously been 'common', open to use by members of local communities. Capitalist development demanded the disruption of the community's access, and thus of its whole basis of life. Property and custom stood opposed, and custom's defenders fought extensive battles, large and small, to protect their own positions against the depradations of the rich and the powerful. Sometimes 'customary' rights and practices survived only because people organised to keep them alive—as when the Vicar of Winkfield in Windsor Forest led his parishioners on a 'parish walk' that deliberately broke down the walls of Richmond Park. The closure of Richmond Park led to a whole series of wall-breakings, public meetings, petitions, actions at law and finally a public victory against the Ranger, Princess Amelia, when the public won the right to climb over stepladders (convenient for the use of elderly women, it was stipulated!) in and out of the Park. We only have parks in London today, Thompson suggests, thanks to the assertion of rights by commoners.[6]

Enclosure and other breaches of customary right provoked resistance, in many forms. Sometimes there were mass actions pulling down of fences and digging up of rabbit warrens, and even pitched battles and riots; sometimes resistance was solitary. The countryside was less successful than urban areas in defending the commons. Here the issue was productive, profitable farmland, and the propertied were less prone to compromise. Custom itself was, as Thompson remarks, 'a place of class conflict, at the interface between agrarian practice and political power'.

More was at stake than just access to land. The meaning of 'property' itself was being transformed and hardened. *Feudal* custom had recognised a host of interwoven claims and reciprocal obligations in relation to land-use. But modern law, representing the 'ulterior rationality of capitalist definitions of property rights'⁷ attacked those claims and obligations head on, breaking them up.

> *It was always a problem to explain the commons within capitalist categories. There was something uncomfortable about them. Their very existence prompted questions about the origin of property and about historical title to land.*⁸

The 18th century jurist, Blackstone, as if to offer a historical preface to Marx's notion of commodity fetishism, entitled the second volume of his *Commentaries* 'Of the Rights of Things'. The very processes by which the labouring classes lost access to land and became a propertyless proletariat, and which Marx discussed in *Capital*, also involved the formation of 'property' in a new and revolutionary-capitalist sense. Blackstone defined property bluntly as '...that sole and despotic dominion which one man claims and exercises over the external things of the world, in total exclusion of the right of any other individual in the universe'. The judges, after due and weighty deliberation, denied the poor the right to glean in Norfolk fields after harvest. Lord Loughborough explained that maintaining such a right was 'inconsistent with the nature of property which imports *exclusive enjoyment*' (my emphasis).⁹

That hard capitalist case for property as a system of exclusion was tied, of course, to arguments about the need to discipline the propertyless, and above all to make them labour. The heart of the issue was, as Thompson puts it succinctly, 'Property in land required a landowner, improving the land required labour, and therefore subduing the earth required also subduing the labouring poor.'¹⁰ If that were not done, how could civilised society subsist?

And when the nephews of civilised society moved abroad to form an empire, they carried these same ideas of property, imposing them everywhere. In the name of 'exclusive property' they reorganised productive processes to fit the capitalist world economy, in a gigantic global process of brigandage, all conducted according to the principles of English law. 'In 1770 Cook claimed the east coast of New South Wales for the Crown, not because it was empty of aborigines but because "we never saw one inch of cultivated land in the whole country"'.¹¹ In New Zealand the Maoris did 'cultivate', but unfortunately did so using various forms of common property; here, a parliamentarian explained, the aim must be:

...the detribalisation of the Natives—to destroy, if it were possible, the principle of communism which ran through the whole of their institutions...and which stood as a barrier in the way of all attempts to amalgamate the native race into our own social and political system.[12]

In 18th century England custom stood against law in 'a place of unqualified class conflict'. The law furthered agrarian capitalist interests, indeed it was those interests.[13] Resisting enclosure and law in the name of custom and common right meant opposing the mechanisms by which labour was being deliberately and forcibly subordinated to capital. Resistance involved posing a distinct and in important respects more humane measure of needs and expectations against the exclusive demands of modern jurisprudence and political economy.

That more humane measure is further explored in Thompson's account of the battles over the price of food, the food riots that litter the 18th century record. Within these riots, Thompson shows, we can descry a set of values and assumptions contrary to those of (capitalist) political economy, and which he terms 'the moral economy of the crowd'. This 'moral economy', in its own way, put the demands of need before those of profit. 'It supposed definite, and passionately held, notions of the common weal'. Those notions, though rooted in an older form of class society, provided the basis for a live critique of those who profiteered in food at times of scarcity. In the texts of political economy, food profiteers (these days termed 'enterprising business executives') are accepted and praised. Eighteenth century people knew them less politely as forestallers, badgers, broggers, hucksters, regraters and the like. And they often acted against them. A series of 'risings of the people', marked by considerable organisation and discipline, along with a host of small collective actions in towns and villages, engaged quite regularly in 'setting the price' of food at a level the crowd considered proper. Sometimes this was undertaken in the name of enforcing old laws which had fallen into disuse. The leaflets calling such demonstrations could be splendid, like this from Stratton (Cornwall) 1801:

> *To all the labouring Men and Tradesmen in the Hundred of Stratton that are willing to save their Wifes and Children from the Dreadfull condition of being STARVED to DEATH by the unfeeling and Griping Farmer... Assemble all emeadiately and march in Dreadfull Array to the Habitations of the Griping Farmer, and Compell them to sell their Corn in the Market, at a fair and reasonable Price...*[14]

Often the 'bargaining by riot' (to adapt a phrase from Eric Hobsbawm) was quite effective, at least in the short term. Magistrates and landowners did sometimes intervene as the crowd demanded, to secure food supplies or control prices. Through much of the 18th century much of this activity was not necessarily especially 'political' in focus, though after the French Revolution the quite common imprecations against the rich and powerful take on a new note, as in the poetic notes of an anonymous letter from Uley (Gloucestershire)—'no King but a Constitution down down down O fatall down high caps and proud hats forever down down...' Or the notice pinned to a tree at Ramsbury (Wiltshire) in 1800:

> Downe with Your Luxzuaras Government both spirital & temperal Or you starve with Hunger. they have stripp you of bread Chees Meate &c &c &c &c &c. Nay even your Lives they have Taken thousands on their Expeditions let the Burbon Family defend their owne Cause and let us true Britons look to Our Selves let us banish Some to Hanover where they came from Downe with your Constitution Arect a republick Or you and your offsprings are to starve the Remainder of our Days dear Brothers will you lay down and die under man eaters and Lave your offspring under that Burden that Blackguard Government which is now eatain you up.

God Save the Poor & down with George III.[15]

By the end of the 18th century, where previously government had often acceded to popular demand, new official voices were heard: the stern tones of Laissez Faire and her sister Exclusive Property, declaring that the troops must deal with riotous crowds who dared interfere with food-prices, or as they termed them 'the nature of things'.

In the 18th century, Thompson reminds us, 'Dearths were real dearths. High prices meant swollen bellies and sick children whose food was coarse bread made up from stale flour...'[16] We don't today in England perhaps feel the pain of food profiteering as it was felt then. But glance at the TV screens with just a slightly widened sense of who 'we' are, and there are still millions of us who feel that pain, and just as angrily. The 'moral economy' of the crowd two centuries ago still has something to offer, especially today when parts of the left talk such non-sense about 'market rationality'.

Even if the crowd in the 18th century invoked historical tradition, a battle for 'moral economy' need by no means be simply backward looking, for, as Thompson remarks, it 'is continuously regenerating itself as anti-capitalist critique, as resistance movement'. Perhaps the term 'moral economy' lacks precision,[17] but the core idea is rooted in strong popular feelings about what is due to people when they are in need, feelings which, as Thompson remarks, 'arise from the elementary exchanges of material life'.[18] The author is himself very careful in his treatment, always holding to a scrupulous historian's sense that the 'moral economy' he discusses belonged in a definite social setting. I'm doubtful that we, his readers, need to be quite so cautious: the priority given to human need in that 'moral economy' shares *something* in common with the more modern idea of 'socialism'.

If one day we can make our own 'moral economy' a dominant active principle of transactions between people, we shall recognise our own history in the 'customary beliefs and values' of the 'plebeian' crowds who are, if not our sisters and brothers, decidedly our very great grandparents. Those who died in its defence, like 54 year old Hannah Smith of Manchester, hanged in 1812 for 'heading up the mob' that brought down the prices of potatoes, butter and milk for several days, belong to us.[19]

Also reprinted here is Thompson's famous essay on 'Time, Work-Discipline and Industrial Capitalism', a meditation on how the capitalist class imposed a new, methodical, machine driven sense of time on us all through clock and bell, fine, wage incentive and school routine. If Karl Marx taught us how capitalists steal our lives in little stitches of time, Edward Thompson shows how they measured it out first for thieving, parcelling, straightening and stretching it, imposing on a customary and 'natural' set of rhythms the new infernal clockwork of the knocker up and the alarm, the time-keeper and the shift system. The new factories were the places, above all, where time itself became a real stake in the class struggle, as it continues to be to this day. How ignorant, declares every bourgeois economic theorist, is Marx's suggestion that *labour time* is the basis of value; and every day in practice the world's employers prove they *know* Marx was right.

Most socialists, I believe, will be delighted with the first 400 pages of Thompson's book. Who will want to quarrel seriously with his brilliant recovery of popular struggles over food prices, the management of time, the enclosure of land? The defence of 'custom' here poses no more problems than does a workplace defence of 'custom and practice' against some employer's assault today. But the last part of the book raises new and very significant issues, which might well provoke argument. Thompson discusses two additional sets of 'customs'. One is the 'wife sale', and the other is 'rough music'. And strange and brutal they sound initially to our civilised ears.

In the wife sale a couple enacts a public ritual. The husband leads his wife into the marketplace with a halter round her neck or waist, and 'sells' her in a parody auction—normally, it seems, to another man who is already primed to make the appropriate bid.[20] Afterwards, often in the pub, the three parties sign a paper together, thereby making the divorce—and often the remarriage[21]—'legal'. How demeaning, and especially to the woman, it all seems!

Then there is 'rough music'. A crowd gathers outside a house making a tremendous rude cacophony, shouting, singing, banging pans, sometimes with more elaborate ritual, to signal its mockery or hostility against some individual or household which has offended against a communal norm. 'Rough music'—'devil's madjic' as one modern witness termed it—went along with such activities as burning people in effigy, carrying victims (or proxies) on a pole or a donkey, sometimes pelting them with mud and tipping them into a pond or ditch. Sometimes these rituals might be fairly friendly (as tying cans to the back of wedding cars usually is), but they could be savage. Such treatment could drive people out of the district, and occasionally no doubt impel them to suicide.

Can we, should we, consider these matters without a shudder? We are dealing here, on the one hand, with 'custom' as popular justice, self government without reference to the state. On the other hand, some forms of this figure in our nightmares, for they include the 'lynch law' of the Ku Klux Klan...

Edward Thompson admits to a certain ambivalence in his views about popular justice. I think I want to disagree with him, and to come down more strongly in its support than he cares to. Let me first present his argument as he develops it around rough music. We must not, he argues, prettify rough music which:

> could...be an excuse for a drunken orgy or for blackmail. It could legitimate the aggression of youths, and (if one may whisper it) youths are not always, in every historical context, protagonists of rationality or of change.

At the same time, he finds himself attracted to much in rough music:

> It is a property of a society in which justice is not wholly delegated or bureaucratised, but is enacted by and within the community... Rough music belongs to a mode of life in which some part of the law belongs still to the community and is theirs to enforce. To this one may assent. It indicates modes of social self-control and the disciplining of certain kinds of violence and anti-social offence (insults to women, child abuse, wife-beating) which in today's cities may be breaking down.[22]

But, he adds, there is a rider. The fact that law belongs to the people does not make it automatically more 'nice' and tolerant, more cosy and folksy. Rough music has been enacted not just against some officious public figure or notorious wife beater, but also, as he notes, against some lonely sexual non-conformist, and the form of the justice meted out could be terrifying, indeed deadly. Rough music and other forms of popular judicial activity could be and have been the instrument of popular bigotry, jingoism, racism. The popular law is 'only as nice and as tolerant as the prejudices and norms of the folk allow'.

In Sussex rough music was visited upon 'pro-Boers', including William Morris's close friend, Georgie Burne-Jones. In Bavaria the last manifestations of **haberfeldtreiben** *were linked to mafia-like blackmail, anti-semitism and, in the final stage, to ascendant Nazism. For some of its victims, the coming of a distanced (if alienated) Law and a bureaucratised police must have felt as a liberation from the tyranny of one's 'own'.*[23]

The argument is a serious one, and most of Thompson's points command assent. Yet I conclude that his ambivalence is misplaced. Certainly, if the heart of socialism is the idea that human beings can democratically and rationally organise their own productive life, above all without benefit of a state standing over them, then matters involving 'custom' and 'popular justice' require serious consideration.

In the 18th century, it seems, the ruling class was compelled to permit some flourishing of popular customary controls over social and economic life. But gradually rough music and other customs declined along with the communities that gave them sustenance, and as the constabulary and other state agencies took over the policing of morality.

The decline itself resulted from a struggle between the bearers of 'law' and 'custom'. The state was jealous and suspicious of popular justice, not least because rough music was dangerous. Not only did the poor judge each other, but they applied the same methods against their betters as a weapon in the class struggle. Rough music was used to enforce collective discipline in strikes, but also an unpopular magistrate was paraded in effigy through the streets and then burned before his house. However the state might dislike rough music in general, it hated it in particular when applied to its own officers. *The First Report of the Constabulary Commissioners*, in 1839, commented:

The right which is thus arrogated of judging...another man's domestic conduct, is certainly characteristic of a rude state of society; when the same measures are applied to...thwarting the operation of the laws of the land, they become of much more serious import. The principle is perfectly Irish, and...contains the germ of resistance to legal order.[24]

This 'Irish...germ of resistance' might be otherwise described as a *partial* effort at what Marx termed 'the subordination of the state to society'.

Thompson's own ambivalence about 'customary justice' is perhaps rooted in the ambivalence about 'law' that he revealed in earlier works, notably his 1975 book, *Whigs and Hunters*. His thought tends sometimes, towards uncritical admiration of 'the rule of law' as 'an unqualified human good'.[25] This position—connected though it is to a very valuable stress on the urgent necessity of defending civil liberties against threats from state authoritarianism—is always at risk of sliding into a subjection to liberalism.[26] One thing that marks liberalism is its assumption of the eternal necessity of a state and of a state-made and state-controlled law.

There is a different perspective on law and its relation to custom which urgently needs further development. The anthropologist Stanley Diamond argues, 'The relation between custom and law is, basically, one of contradiction, not continuity'.[27] 'Law' does not exist as a disembodied set of special (and in some writers' hands meritorious) rules and procedures, but is always an emanation of state power. Who says 'rule of law' says 'rule of state'. The rise of 'rule of state' is essential to class society. The development of the 'rule of law' has not occurred on some higher plane than the rest of history. Law has not, in the largest sense, been an instrument of equality and freedom, but of exploitation and subordination.

Involved in the emergence of 'legal order' was a substitution: in place of previous customary organisation came the principle of subordination to a state and its rules. Custom was necessarily the property of the people; law was not. The two stood in as much opposition at the birth of class society as they do in Thompson's account of 18th century England.[28] 'State rule' supposes the development of a power apart from, superior to, battening down on and exploiting everyday society. The first law of the state was always the subordination of society to itself. It took over custom's rules and powers and and turned them into 'law'—in order better to secure the means to control and tax society. All the elements in the growth of the early state, wherever we find it, were 'occasions for the development of civil law'.[29] When states took over justice, the process was one in which a class interposed itself into an existing system of popular justice, monopolised that social power to itself, altered it and removed it from popular control. Law and state are forms of alienation, which consists not simply in the production of surplus value for our exploiters, but also and equally in our loss of control over society and its rules.

Justice is not the invention of 'law'. Long before ever any form of state existed, there was 'justice'. That is, there were rules about right and wrong, ways of teaching these, means of rectifying wrongs and dealing with wrongdoers. 'Society' without 'justice' (along with 'morality', 'rights', etc) is inconceivable—who says society says morals, rules and procedures. But society without 'state' is perfectly conceivable. Against any tendency to celebrate the rule of law Diamond's words are a useful corrective:

The legal order, which Plato idealised, is, as Taylor maintained and Marx understood, synonymous with the power of the state... If revolutions are the

acute, episodic signs of civilisational disorder, the rule of law, in seven mil-
lenia of political society, from Sumer or Akkad to New York or Moscow, has
been the chronic symptom of the disorder of institutions...we come to under-
stand law as the antonym and not the synonym of order.[30]

This, of course, is not how the state presents itself. The state's case is
that we can't possibly make our lives safe without it. Will not society
fall into endless pillage, murder, rape and anarchy without a *police*
force? Thus do the police justify their part. Their 'mission' is to protect
society from its own incipient collapse into anarchy. Since society is
unaware of the real dangers facing it, the police, like Judge Dredd, must
be empowered to act to save us from our own ignorance and foolishness.
Innocent and incapable society must trust those who know, and empower
them to do its dirty work.[31] There is of course a plain response to this:
given the rising costs of policing and imprisoning, why are crime levels
apparently rising inexorably? The more we spend on law, it seems, the
less safe we are. Why are these guardians of order so massively *ineffec-*
tive?

Against popular justice, it is alleged that it has been associated with
appalling crimes. The charge is, of course, completely true. But is that a
case for state justice? We can grant that a defence of rough music must
take account of the Ku Klux Klan; but equally those who speak for state
justice have to answer, not just for the Birmingham Six, but also for
Auschwitz and the Gulag. Those who were subjected to rough music
were often deeply and permanently marked by the experience, but then
surely the suicide rate in prisons must be part of a balanced equation?[32]

A one-sided 'pro-law' case against 'custom' and 'popular justice' ultimately involves a deeply elitist judgement that 'reason' and rationality
are the property of a minority located at the top of society, and that the
bottom of society is indeed just that—not a thinking part, but something
to be sat upon. Such ideas, of course, deeply impregnate much that
passes for 'democratic theory' in our culture.[33]

To accept the state and law, and to make their acceptance the bound-
ary of what is possible in politics, is to accept the exclusion of the mass
of the population from the direct determination of their own lives. It is to
accept the notion that a ruling class is necessary and good for society.
That is, it is to accept hierarchy and subordination as eternal necessities
of the human condition, and to assert the impossibility of any democracy
deeper than the shallow parliamentary form we now possess. It is to
accept human exploitation and dignify 'injustice' as 'justice'.

Questions about the social and political forms in which justice is
enacted do not belong solely to the distant past. In August 1980 in
Poland, during the rise of Solidarnosc, workers occupied the Port of
Gdynia. In taking control they took over responsibility for themselves,

and for the property there. One of their rules was: No thieving from the cargoes. And what happened when a worker broke the rules?

> *There were some general cargo-pallets under the fence near the cross, placed there in order to enable us to look over the fence to see our fellow shipyard workers (in the Paris Commune yards next door). The offender would stand on the pallets and men would hoot and call abuses at them. That was the greatest punishment, to which thieves and traitors were sentenced.*[34]

In every significant revolutionary and potentially revolutionary movement in the 20th century the issue of popular justice has re-emerged. Inherent in the confrontations of social revolution is the question, whose justice is to prevail, Theirs or Ours? That question has all manner of ramifications. 'Justice' is a term whose meaning only exists in a definite social context. To ask, 'What is justice?' is is to ask what 'moral economy' is being applied, what access-rights to property are provided, what needs are recognised, what obligations and moral rules are enforced, what procedures are used to determine responsibility. It is to ask, above all, who is determining these matters, and how? If the term 'class justice' has any meaning, all these matters are implicated in it.

I am suggesting a line of argument which many will find controversial. My suggestion is that, implicit within 'custom' as it has survived and transformed itself within class society and with all its contradictions, there is a kind of partial anticipation of socialist society. Engels found within the 'gentile constitution' of pre-class society, a significant vantage point from which to criticise 'civilisation'—without, of course, denying the need to build on the achievements of that same civilisation. I am offering a slightly similar case. There is more to 'custom' than mere quaintness.

My argument for 'custom' concerns both its form and something of its content. Consider first the wife sale. One feature of the custom is immediately striking: control over it belongs directly to the participants. This is true whether we judge the custom 'nice' or 'nasty', utterly degrading to women or not (and Thompson has some sensible remarks on *that*). There is a 'play script' which is followed in broad outlines. But the participants themselves (who include the audience in the marketplace) determine how the play shall be done, what variations are appropriate, who shall be humiliated and who treated with kindness and support. A customary ritual belongs to its actors. They may play it in as enlightened or as crude a fashion as they themselves are persuaded.

Suppose we do find it degrading. Had we been there, we could—like the participants then—have varied the script, developed the form. We could have refused to play, as some did. We could have cheered the woman, as some did. We could have execrated, or sympathised with, the

losing husband or the lover who was gaining a wife—as some did. We
might even have suggested some less objectionable way of 'registering'
the divorce in our community. Each choice would have had its effects,
some good, some not. But the whole thing would have remained—for
good or ill—under our own slightly messy but collective control. An attractive element in the wife sale ritual is something we hardly notice: no
one seeks 'permission' to divorce and remarry from any lord, any
church, any state and its law. The matter is in the hands of the
participants—and their community.

Most divorces are painful, messy affairs. This 18th century way of
handling them would not suit us today. But in the relatively close community of a small market town a divorce was always going to be the
neighbours' business, the object of gossip and perhaps humilitation. The
public wife sale gave the participants the—not necessarily happy—
chance to enact the change in their relations publicly, and to reveal their
mutual agreement to it. The event was not always good humoured, and
might be very degrading, especially—but not only—for the wife.

The wife sale grew up in a definite setting, where the church courts no
longer had the same power over sexual conduct, and where the state had
not yet asserted its law. Here was a ritual drawing its imagery from the
marketplace, but in a setting where the 'plebeian' culture had a degree of
autonomy from the polity. In important senses, the community's recognition and assent to the divorce was needed. Was the ritual so bad, compared with the state law that finally opposed it, and that gaoled
participants for 'bigamy'? What will a future age make of 'our' divorce
courts, where the participants lie to the judge, and lawyers fatten on our
miseries?

As Thompson shows in his discussion of rough music, popular justice
can be very rough and ready, but it has the unique characteristic of being
open to instant amendment and immediate rebalancing, in a way that
state law can rarely match. Custom stands in a condition of permanent
referendum and amendment. It has no self enclosed majesty to defend,
even if it is sometimes riven with unappealing prejudice. Custom is a
form of self-government, and self government can never rise higher than
popular opinion, with all its contradictions. Thompson's remark about
rough music applies more widely to popular culture:

> *The forms are pliant. Indeed, they have great flexibility. Even in the same*
> *region similar forms can be used to express a good-humoured jest or to*
> *invoke inexorable community antagonism.'* [35]

Popular norms, with their enforcement mechanisms, undergo change,
are subject to argument. New balances of power develop between men

and women, as new issues and arguments come to the fore. Norms, morals, customs represent a key sphere for 'political' intervention.

Thompson provides a nice example of the possibilities of change. The earlier 18th century evidence, he suggests, points to rough music being directed 'patriarchally' at women accused of being scolds and husband-beaters. That is, rough music was used to keep women 'in their place'. But in one community in early 19th century Glamorgan, the women refused to join a rough music procession aimed at a wife who had beaten her husband: they took measures of counter-demonstration:

'They remained indoors and "mocked at (the men) through the windows", while some "collected to scoff" at the house of the victims and "poured out a din of hoots and yells" to drown the rough music.'[36] One wonders, along with Edward Thompson, if other communities witnessed a similar turning of the tide. The point is that 'norms' do get shifted, arguments are rebalanced. *Someone* in Glamorgan went round and said, 'Let's us women do things differently, let's not in this case follow the men...' Sometimes, Thompson reports, rough music was employed with 'wit and intelligence', sometimes with 'prejudice (against innovators, "deviants" and outsiders) and rancour'. 'The rites are like a keyboard that can be played lightly, satirically, or struck brutally.'[37] How the rites are played is a function of what people think, feel and argue among themselves.

The socialist case depends on an assumption about the majority in society, namely that it is 'reason-able'. Not, decidedly, that 'the workers are always right', any more than 'one cannot be correct against the party'. The case for a huge expansion of democratic control in the sphere of justice, culture and morals (without which the case for socialism is empty) rests on a simple assertion: that the majority is open to argument, has a variable readiness at different moments to discuss, to listen, to argue, to think, to change its mind in larger or smaller measure. In short, human beings are just that and not dumb animals or machines (which is how the ruling class tend to view the majority, since in practice that is how they use us).

Part of the value of Thompson's work lies in his capacity to reveal the 'positive' aspect of the customs of the oppressed and exploited. Within them lies, more or less deeply buried, something of the *form* of a stateless society, as a potential. They embody—no doubt crudely, and in contradictory form—notions of the 'moral' which are actually higher in important respects than those of bourgeois culture: notions of communal support, solidarity, friendship, space for play as well as work. It is said that within every fat person is a thin one struggling to get out; even within the culture of class society, likewise, something opposite is 'struggling to get out'.

This is not to deny the deeply problematical aspect of 'custom', which has allowed wife beating and put women in the kitchen. 'Custom' has been attached to racist prejudice, to religion, to hierarchy and to localism. 'Custom' is inconceivable without 'tradition', and that in turn is linked to class society.[38]

Rough music was visited on people for offences we find deeply disturbing: conjugal infidelity as well as wife or husband battering, nagging as well as rape[39] and theft, unpopular marriages and remarriages as well as scabbing and informing, homosexuality as well as ill treatment of children. 'This "folk"', writes Edward Thompson, 'was not perfect nor pretty nor was it empty of all norms.' And who can disagree? Thompson is absolutely correct to reject any glamorisation of 'custom' or popular morality; in their name all manner of dreadful things have been done. But the argument should be less about form—and about a contrast with 'the rule of law'—and more about content. Odious customs are odious not for being customary but for the ideas and practices they embody.

There are no morals or customs independently of social context. What Edward Thompson says about rough music is also true of the wife sale and other customs: they are in themselves indicators of sexual norms and marital roles, and of the way in which private and 'personal' relations are conditioned by norms imposed by the community in which couples quarrel or love.[40]

The advantage of custom over law is the advantage of community over state. With a community—as distinct from a state—we are as much part of it as anyone else is. If there is anything we can intervene in and shape, it is a 'community'. Of course, a 'community' cannot be discussed independently of class, any more than morals and customs can. Communities are sites both of struggle and of appeasement, where culture and custom, habits and morals are formed in an unavoidable *association* between classes. Classes depend economically upon each other even as they struggle. The ideas and habits of classes are shaped in part by others. In their mutual struggle and association each generation imbibes and further develops its forbears' ambiguous heritage. Popular culture is quite as contradictory, we might say, as the consciousness of the 'man in the mass' that Antonio Gramsci discussed, combining elements of the caveman and the most advanced philosophy.

So it is not surprising that, as Thompson suggests, elements of rough music ritual were taken over from earlier class justice, in the shape of church and state punishments. It was the Church Hierarchical that prescribed the naked parading of 'lewd women', the state that prescribed the stocks. Thompson notes that the symbolism of public execution irradiated popular culture in the 18th century, and the memory of public burnings (of heretics and witches) survived too. The popular culture, in short, did not develop in total autonomy from ruling class influence. But then what popular culture in class society ever could?

'Custom' seems to be a backward force, contrary to 'Enlightenment' and 'Rationality'. But the desire to conserve *anything* is not necessarily a sign of political reaction. The difficulty, in a sense, lies in disentangling within as complex an issue as a 'custom', a 'habit', a 'ritual' or indeed a 'moral rule' what is and what is not valuable and worth preserving and developing. Shall we abandon the celebration of birthdays? Shall we stop having funerals? Shall we simply, as good atheists, stop celebrating Christmas? Or shall we rather, as Leon Trotsky[41] proposed, seek to transform customs in more attractive forms which will tend to separate them from their connections with hierarchy, submissiveness, division and the like and connect them with new and emerging visions of human community and freedom?

If we loathe a specific custom, or the manner of its celebration, how should we seek to combat it? In some cases, to be sure, we might choose to use legal repression. But repression is often not a very *convincing* and transforming argument. And nothing is so ineffective as 'moralism'; few socialists would fancy being tagged, like David Underdown's Puritans, as those with 'the duty of the godly to reform their less enlightened neighbours'.[42] If custom is not fixed and unchangeable, and if the problem of 'customs' and 'morals' is not their abolition but their transformation, the significance of 'custom' is that its form—its character as popular property—makes it open to a specific kind of change through the internal development of the people whose partial life-expression it is.

Where, ultimately, is it more important to win an argument against racism? In the public bar of the King's Arms or privately before the king's throne, in the post office or parliament, in the bus garage or the CBI? In the long run the former is decisive, above all to the degree that it becomes the real focus of political power.

Perhaps the specificity of 'custom' comes out, ultimately, in the view we form of how to change it where we dislike it. Trotsky's view of how family life might be reformed is, in this respect, impeccably sensitive. While he urges that the material resources for a better family and community life must be developed, he insists on the need for great caution before there is any direct state interference with the domestic world. The key thing, he insists, is that the 'prison-like silence surrounding our present-day customs' must be broken—in order that they may be rationally discussed, argued over, and amended *by their owners*. For, ultimately, it is the fact that customs are directly popular property which requires that they be amended 'from within', by those who own and live them.

Custom is often merely local in its roots, its recognitions and its powers, while socialism speaks of the formation of a universal society. And again the objection is true: the elements of popular control, common experience and moral economy we find within 'popular culture' (in all their contradictory combination with fateful submissiveness, narrowness, suspicion and the like) lack power unless they are joined up with a universalising rational collective political argument that addresses people not as members of face to face communities but as members of the world proletariat. Trotsky called socialist revolution:

...a mad rebellion in the name of the conscious, rational, purposive and dynamic principle of life, against the elemental, senseless, biological automatism of life, that is, against the peasant roots of our old Russian history, against its aimlessness, its non-teleological character.[43]

Of course, the absolute precondition for the adequate transformation of morals and customs is the establishment of workers' power. Without theory no revolutionary practice; without power no revolutionary customs. Only as popular democratic power and a classless society develop can we even discover how far, freely, a people can develop their own potentialities and their morals and their customs to embody the highest reason.

Engels looked forward to the day when the whole machinery of the state, and its law, would be 'put into the Museum of Antiquities, by the side of the spinning wheel and the bronze axe'. In its place, he argued, would come 'the society that will organise production on the basis of a free and equal association of the producers'.[44] The working of such a society will depend on the combined wisdom and foolishness of the customs of its people, and the quality of the arguments among them for justice, morals and all the rest.

Near the start of his fascinating book Edward Thompson presents a case for the *relevance* of his studies. We should have no quarrels about it: 'We shall not ever return to pre-capitalist human nature, yet a reminder of its alternative needs, expectations and codes may renew our sense of our nature's range of possibilities'.[45] But even there his tone is a touch ambivalent, defensive and uncertain. Might we, he asks, through struggle make over our own human nature, its needs and expectations, in a new form, in a newly made, more economically rational and culturally satisfying world? 'I do not think this is likely to happen', he concludes with a touch of miserabilism in the night. There is perhaps no point in arguing about what is likely to happen. But it is worth arguing about whether such changes are possible, whether they are worth fighting for, and what might be the conditions under which we could make some real progress in such a direction. That argument, still, is what being a socialist is about.

Notes

My thanks to Ewa Barker, John Charlton, Sue Clegg and John Rees for stimulating comment on an earlier draft. It is customary to note that those one thanks are not responsible. Here, at least, they can unstintingly celebrate custom.

1   In his earlier *Whigs and Hunters*, (1975) Thompson suggested 18th century government had 'the sick quality of a "banana republic".'
2   E P Thompson, *Customs in Common* (London, 1991), p45.
3   Ibid, p64.
4   Ibid, p69.
5   Ibid, p6. Thompson quotes an early 20th century folklorist, Gomme: 'These customs, rites and beliefs are mostly kept alive by tradition... They owe their preservation partly to the fact that great masses of people do not belong to the civilisation which towers over them and which is never of their own creation' (cit 6).
6   It matters: London has 22.8 square metres of park per head of population, Tokyo has just two. (Nigel Harris, 'The New Untouchables: The International Migration of Labour', *International Socialism*, 8). These matters are now given occasional semi-official recognition, as in the following comment on the 1932 Mass Trespass on Kinder Scout: 'Many people have since questioned the need for, and effectiveness of, the Mass Trespass, which was followed by others that received much less publicity. But there can be no doubt that it proved to be one of the most important catalysts for the National Parks and access to the countryside legislation which followed World War II.' (The Ordnance Survey *Peak District Leisure Guide*, Ordnance Survey/Automobile Association, 1987, p12.)
7   E P Thompson, op cit, p133.
8   Ibid, p159.
9   Ibid, p139. It was no good appealing to biblical authority, the Law Lord added, for 'the law of Moses' had been superseded by 'Christian dispensation' and that recognised no *legal obligation* to relieve the poor, only a 'religious duty'...
10   Ibid, p167.
11   Ibid, p165.
12   Ibid, p166.
13   A footnote, p176, cites the *Poor Man's Guardian* of 1835: 'Property is but the creation of law. Whoever makes the law has the power of appropriating the national wealth. If they did not make the law, they would not have the property.'
14   E P Thompson, op cit, pp234-235.
15   Ibid, pp248-249.
16   Ibid, p256.
17   As Thompson suggests, it's better than 'other terms (such as "dialectical asymetrical reciprocity") which we might otherwise be clobbered with'—p344.
18   Ibid, p350.
19   Ibid, p334. One day, when Manchester has a council of labour instead of just a Labour Council, we could honour Hannah Smith at least with a street name. But then bourgeois Manchester, which has a Free Trade Hall, has yet to name its Peterloo Sports Stadium.
20   It is perhaps only in Thomas Hardy's fictional *Mayor of Casterbridge* that a stranger buys the wife.

21   There are a few cases where a woman's kin 'buy' her: an arranged divorce, Thompson suggests, taking a woman back from an unsatisfactory marriage.

22   E P Thompson, op cit, p530.

23   Ibid, pp530-531.

24   See ibid, p521.

25   E P Thompson, *Whigs and Hunters: The Origins of the Black Act* (New York, 1975), p266. In the name of that unqualified human good, Thompson urged us, against revolutionary optimism, to watch out for a century or two 'before you cut your hedges down'—an odd and surely deliberate choice of image for a socialist historian so sensitive to the erection of hedges and fences, to enclosure and the abolition of common right, as central symbols of property's dominance over popular need.

26   See the very thoughtful critique of Thompson in B Fine, *Democracy and the Rule of Law*, (London, 1984), pp169-189.

27   S Diamond, 'The Rule of Law Versus the Order of Custom' in Robert Paul Wolff (ed), *The Rule of Law* (New York, 1971), p117.

28   The point was recognised long ago by Engels, who wrote in *The Origin of the Family, Private Property and the State* of 'the irreconcilable opposition of gentile society to the state'.

29   S Diamond, op cit, p129, cites the learned opinion of the great historical jurist Stubbs on the Middle Ages: 'It was mainly for the sake of the profits that early justice was administered at all'. I think it was Perry Anderson who remarked that feudal justice was 'the ordinary name for power'.

30   Ibid, pp135, 136, 138.

31   See eg R Reiner, *The Politics of the Police* (Brighton, 1985), pp88-91.

32   I wrote this review over two days. The first day, 28 February 1992, I read in the *Guardian* that Kevin McCauley, aged 35, of the Isle of Man, committed suicide after being interrogated by the police about homosexual activities. A Manx gay activist accused the police of murder: 'Kevin's death was the result of his interrogation', he said. Next day the paper led with the story of Jacqueline Fletcher, aged 28, jailed for life after *confessing* to murdering her baby son, and released after four years when it was proved that the baby had died of cot death syndrome. Has there ever been a time when 'British justice' has sounded more like a contradiction in terms?

33   There's an incisive critique of this pattern of theorising in P Bachrach, *The Theory of Democratic Elitism* (London, 1967).

34   J Gajda, 'August 1980 As I Saw It' in W W Adamski (ed), *Sisyphus Sociological Studies, vol 3: Crises and Conflicts, The Case of Poland 1980-1981* (Warsaw, 1982), p242) from C Barker, *Festival of the Oppressed*, (Bookmarks, 1986), p24. Anyone interested in this whole question might also care to look at the materials on popular courts in Portugal and 'Pasagarda law' in Brazil discussed in B de Sousa Santos, 'Popular Justice, Dual Power and Socialist Strategy' in B Fine et al (eds), *Capitalism and the Rule of Law: From deviancy theory to Marxism* (London, 1979).

35   E P Thompson, op cit, p482.

36   Ibid, p511.

37   Ibid, pp514-515.

38   Though 'tradition', like 'custom', is a pliant and supple form, capable of being *developed* in all manner of ways. See E J Hobsbawm and T Ranger (ed), *The Invention of Tradition* (Cambridge, 1983).

39   And also for what was regarded as excessive punishment—execution—for rape. E P Thompson, op cit, p517.

40   Nor is this a matter only of past history. A very 'liberated' student told me that her relations with boyfriends are constrained by what she only half laughingly termed 'the moral majority', ie her friends' gossip and comment.

41 L Trotsky, *Problems of Life* (1924) (Ceylon, 1962). Trotsky's whole pamphlet—whose target is the backwardness of Russian popular moral life—is nicely sensitive to the real complexities of custom. Thanks to the separate urgings of Sue Clegg and John Rees, I read Trotsky almost simultaneously with D Underdown's fascinating *Revel, Riot and Rebellion: Popular Politics and Culture in England 1603-1660* (Oxford, 1985). Underdown's theme is the Puritan assault on popular custom, and the way that many agrarian communities reacted in defence of their 'revels' by turning towards the Royalist party in the 1650s. The contrast between bourgeois and socialist revolutionary practice is in some ways encapsulated in the difference between Puritan and Bolshevik. The Puritans sought to repress by force all religious and aesthetic-recreational practices other than their own; Trotsky seeks to transcend and transform custom, not to root it out by state power. But then the Puritan project, ultimately, was the subordination of human society to alien forces; the socialist project is human self emancipation.

42 D Underdown, op cit, p275.

43 L Trotsky, *Literature and Revolution* (Bookmarks, 1991), p140.

44 F Engels, *The Origin of the Family, Private Property and the State* in Marx/Engels, Selected Works (Moscow, 1958), Vol 2, p322.

45 E P Thompson, op cit, p15.

Revolutionary witness

*A review of **Arthur Ransome in Revolutionary Russia** (Redwords, 1992) £12.95*

SHEILA McGREGOR

> *By the nature of things it has so happened that practically all the foreign ob-*
> *servers of events in Russia have belonged to the privileged classes in their*
> *respective countries, and have been accustomed to associate with the privi-*
> *leged classes in Russia. They have consequently found it difficult to escape*
> *from their class in judging the story happening before their eyes.*[1]

The Russian Revolution was always going to be reviled by those who stood to lose from workers seizing power in society. But until the complete collapse of Communism in 1989-91, there were also those who, in however distorted a form, would defend the October revolution.

Today, it is common currency on the left as well as the right to argue that the October revolution was a mistake, and that the best any of us can hope for are limited bourgeois freedoms. Whilst welcoming the collapse of Communism this has left those of us who defend October with a monumental task. So the reprinting by Redwords of a pamphlet and two books as *Arthur Ransome in Revolutionary Russia* could not be more timely. Ransome was never a Marxist or a revolutionary. He was caught up in the revolution by accident when, after a miserable marriage, he travelled to Russia in 1914. Today he is known as a writer of children's books. Hopefully he will now become known for his eyewitness accounts of the revolution in Russia.

These writings from 1918, 1919 and 1920 not only reflect Ransome's own enthusiasm for the revolution but provide a snapshot of the course of the revolution, its workings, problems and successes. All three serve to refute some of the most basic arguments advanced by the right and now parroted by the left, arguments which are not new but which were spawned by the opponents of the revolution at the time.

Today the picture portrayed of the revolution is essentially this: okay, so the Tsar had to go in February, but after that the Bolsheviks hijacked the revolution and organised a coup against the will of the masses. Hence they dispersed the Constituent Assembly in January 1918 because they were only a minority and proceeded to fight a civil war to retain power in which they had to resort to unspeakable mass terror precisely because they were an isolated minority.

The importance of Ransome's writings is that as an eyewitness writing first for the *Daily News* and then for *The Manchester Guardian* he not only refutes that account but gives a glimpse of what the revolution really meant to the mass of people. Ransome's own enthusiasm for the Bolshevik revolution bursts out of the first pamphlet, 'A Letter to America', reprinted here as 'The Truth about Russia', which he wrote for an American audience in 1918. This opens with a quote from Emerson:

> *If there is any period one would desire to be born in—is it not the age of revolution; when the old and new stand side by side, and admit of being compared; when the energies of all men are searched by fear and by hope; when the historic glories of the old can be compensated by the rich possibilities of the new era? This time, like all times, is a very good one, if we but know what to do with it.*[2]

He concludes the pamphlet thus:

> *These men who have made the Soviet government in Russia, if they must fail, will fail with clean shields and clean hearts, having striven for an ideal which will live beyond them. Even if they fail, they will none the less have written a page of history more daring than any other which I can remember in the history of humanity.*[3]

For Ransome the revolution was about ideals, and about daring to make history. He himself was generous spirited enough to get caught up in the infectiousness of a real revolution. But the revolution also inspired him to try to explain it to others blinded either by ignorance, propaganda or class. Not that he thought that the Bolsheviks were angels. He didn't.

Nor was he blind to the tough reality of revolution, particularly in the conditions of the time. But he preferred the revolution to its opponents. He understood only too clearly the consequences of a victory by the counter-revolutionary forces in Russia.

On the strength of his reporting of Russian affairs, Ransome was sent an invitation to attend the first meeting of the Soviet of Workmen's and Soldiers' Deputies, the body which emerged at the same time as the Provisional Government. Ransome's verdict on the soviet was twofold: firstly that the soviet truly represented the people's will, and secondly that this new form of democracy was to be welcomed:

> *I do not think I shall ever again be so happy in my life as I was during those first days when I saw working men and peasant soldiers sending representatives of their class and not of mine. I remembered Shelley's*
> *'Shake your chains to earth like dew*
> *Which in sleep had fallen on you*
> *Ye are many—they are few.'*
> *and wondered that this thing had not come to pass before.*[4]

So widespread today is the belief that Lenin and Trotsky simply organised a coup that some of Ransome's observations to the contrary seem almost funny, like the fact that all the orders for the insurrection were made openly over the telephone! But then Trotsky and the Military Committee of the Petrograd Soviet, who organised the insurrection, knew not only that the Bolsheviks had been overwhelmingly elected the majority in the soviets from the beginning of September but that the masses of peasants wanted land and peace and that the Provisional Government would not give it them. They also knew that after the defeat of Kornilov the counter-revolutionary forces were in no position to stop the insurrection.

Precisely because he understood the soviets to be a superior form of mass participatory democracy, acutely sensitive to the political pulse of those represented within them, Ransome dismisses the arguments about the Constituent Assembly as part of what he calls 'the necessary opportunism of all parties in a time of revolution'.[5] In other words, those who shouted most about the dismissal of the Constituent Assembly in January 1918 themselves had failed to convene it for eight months for fear it would lean too much towards the socialists.

Ransome's argument that the question of the Constituent Assembly 'was for neither party an end in itself. It was a tool, not a task. It was thrown away when further use of it would have damaged the purpose for which it was invented'[6] is surely borne out by the fact that the hue and cry outside Russia over the dismissal of the Constituent Assembly was accompanied by almost complete silence inside the country. Or, as

Ransome so nicely puts it, 'Not anywhere in Russia did the indifferent mass stir in protest. The assembly died, like the Tsardom and the Coalition before it. Not any one of the three showed in the manner of its dying that it retained any right to live.'[7]

Isn't it time that others took heed of one simple fact—that the masses who got rid of the Tsar, refused to continue fighting an imperialist war, seized the land from the landlords and took power in the factories preferred soviet government over a Constituent Assembly?

Ransome's understanding that the new soviet government was deeply rooted in the masses led him not only to campaign against intervention by the Allies, particularly England, but also to write a damning indictment of White terrorism and locate the Bolsheviks' use of terror clearly in the context of the pressures of the civil war. In a private letter written at the end of November 1918 to Gardiner, editor of the liberal *Daily News* for which he was correspondent at the time, Ransome writes:

The result of the mass of the people being opposed to the counter-revolution has been to compel the counter-revolution to support themselves by terrorism: that is by wholesale arrests, and by wholesale killings. I do not want to insist on this point, but merely mention Poltsva, Kiev, Ekaterinoder, Novo-Rossisk, Rostov, and Novotcherkassk, as the scenes of killings, the aggregate of which makes the no less abominable killings in Moscow a mere bucket of blood in an ocean.[8]

Ransome was adamant that the counter-revolution would be totally incapable of garnering an army to support it and would therefore be dependent on outside forces to sustain it. Ransome lays out for Gardiner what this would mean:

But, with the occupation of Moscow, even if that is accomplished far more easily than I think possible, the real work of intervention will be only beginning. You must remember that through the soviets hundreds of thousands of workmen throughout Russia have tasted political power: hundreds of thousands have begun to live an active political life; thousands are employed in responsible positions by the government they feel to be their own. Denikin, Sazonov, Ivanov, Dolgorukov, Miliukov, and the rest will soon put a stop to that; so that the whole of Russia will, from a police point of view, be a network of dissatisfied persons who must be rooted out.[9]

Just as the need for the Whites to use mass terror to break the soviet system of government is obvious to Ransome, so it is obvious to him: 'Jewish pogroms if any, will be, as they always have been, instigated by the reactionaries.'[10] Because Ransome grasps the central class conflict at the heart of the civil war, he also dismisses any idea of a 'middle course' between soviet government and counter-revolution. Hence he writes to Gardiner: 'The position is much clearer than it has been before. It is not a question between the Bolsheviks and the rest of the revolution. It is a question between the revolution and a counter-revolution, between the Soviet Republic and a monarchy.'[11]

One of the chapters in Ransome's book *Six Weeks in Russia* is devoted to interviews with the different opposition parties—Left SRs, Mensheviks and Right SRs—in order to illustrate his point that, much as they may all have opposed the Bolsheviks and their concept of workers' revolution, nevertheless they would defend the soviets against the counter-revolution.

Most people have a picture of the 'Red Terror' similar to that of the Gestapo and Nazi Germany, complete with the notorious 'knock in the night', a picture reinforced by the reality of Stalinism. Ransome devotes one chapter in *Six Weeks* to the question of the Cheka and the seriousness with which the Bolsheviks took the question of the use of terror in defence of the soviets.

It is worth remembering when reading this chapter that Ransome was not only a reporter, but an English reporter, recording the debate in the Executive Committee of the soviet in the midst of a civil war where England was one of the main countries backing the Whites and counter-revolution. Ransome records Dzerzhinsky, leader of the Cheka, making clear that:

> *The law of war by which meeting him on the field of battle, the soldier had a right to kill his enemy without trial, no longer held good. The situation was now that of peace, where each offender must have his guilt proved before a court. Therefore the right of sentencing was removed from the Extraordinary Commission.*[12]

Furthermore the relationship between the use of terror and the threat of counter-revolution is made clear in the following: 'If, through unforeseen circumstances, the old conditions should return, they intended that the dictatorial powers of the Commission should be restored to it until those conditions ceased.'[13] Ransome then lists some of the provisions for justice introduced by Dzerzhinsky such as the establishment of revolutionary tribunals which could take no longer than a month on investigations and for a trial to follow within 48 hours of an investigation.

For those who are firmly convinced that the Bolsheviks only won the civil war because of their superior use of terror (an odd thought given Saddam Hussein's success rate in the recent Gulf War) the following account by Kerkmasov, president of the Daghestan Soviet Republic, can perhaps shed some light on the matter. In a discussion with Ransome, Kerkmasov recalls:

*In 1917 after the first revolution in Russia there began an agrarian move-
ment in Daghestan, peasants against landlords. The whole of Daghestan was
more or less anti-Kerensky. On the one side were the general officers and
landowners who wanted something further right, on the other were the peasants who very decidedly wanted something further left. The first peasant conference in Daghestan in August 1917 showed this clearly. It was Bolshevik
already before the October Revolution.*[14]

Daghestan was beset by three lots of troops—Turkish, English and
Whites. Kerkmasov described the impact of the English:

*The British then used to fly over us with aeroplanes dropping proclamations
and then dropping bombs. The bombs did not do much damage, but the
proclamations helped us a lot... The proclamations were signed by an English
general, I think R Rawlinson, and they told us that Denikin was getting his
tanks and uniforms and aeroplanes from England. Therefore, they said, in
fighting Denikin, you are fighting England. Well now that was exactly what
we had been saying ourselves. We had been saying just that, that Denikin was
not fighting for Russia, but on behalf of English and other capitalists. And
here comes an English aeroplane and obligingly tells the people that the
Communists are in the right.*[15]

Not only does Kerkmasov explain why the Whites lost, his description of relations between his mountainous, predominantly Muslim republic in the Caucusus and the centre, Moscow, is a treat:

*Daghestan is actually federated with Russia, whereas Azerbaijan is allied.
We have our own constitution, adjusted to local needs and characteristics.
We are mountaineers and Mohammedans, we have no proletariat, no factories in the ordinary sense. Our mountains do not supply enough bread to last
us more than six months in the year. We grow cattle, and besides that our
craftsmen work in their own homes. By exchange with our neighbours we can
live well enough, but obviously the rules that are all right for Moscow would
not always work for us.*[16]

And how did these Communists deal with the Cheka? Kerkmasov:

*We had trouble with Chekists, (members of the Cheresvychaika or Extraordi-
nary Commission) who came down and said we were not revolutionary
enough and wanted to mix in what they did not understand; I arrested the
head of them, and sent him back to Moscow as a present, said that they could
keep that fruit to themselves. One or two others we had to shoot. But they
begin to understand that revolution in a Mohammedan country must take its*

own time and go its own way. We have shown its reality too well for them to doubt us by our three years of struggle against the counter-revolutionaries.[17]

Such was the reality of the right of self determination in Lenin's time and the robustness of debate in the Bolshevik Party. Ransome knew that the Bolsheviks made mistakes but he also knew that their organisation was far from monolithic and that they were not afraid to admit their mistakes and set about correcting them. In a different discussion altogether with Eliava, the man being sent to Turkestan to try to correct the mistakes made by Bolsheviks who had been overzealous, overbearing, insensitive and stupid, Ransome records Eliava saying:

In Turkestan, I shall have the same sort of difficulty. There too much harm has been done by Bolsheviks who have tried to introduce the same regime that suits Moscow in a country ready for nothing of the sort. For example some idiot tried to nationalise the fruit gardens. As if it were possible to do anything of the sort. The natural result would be a general spoiling of the fruit. The conditions there are wholly unlike those of the industrial centres of European Russia. There are no big towns to count. There is no proletariat in the proper sense of the word. It is considered an honour to be a merchant. Of a merchant people say 'Ah, he must be a clever fellow.' Almost everybody owns land, and there is very little poverty. All I hope to do is to work for a regime that shall be satisfactory to the people, that shall not impede their development, and that shall be friendly to Russia and able and willing to cooperate with Russia.[18]

The accepted picture of Bolshevik Russia as a completely undemocratic monolith is constantly belied by Ransome in both volumes. In *Six Weeks*, one chapter is devoted to a discussion in the Executive Committee of the Soviet about the declaration from the Right SRs about their past mistakes which also called on their supporters to help overthrow 'the usurping government in Siberia and elsewhere'. Not everyone was so keen to readmit these people to the Soviet, given their past record helping the Whites. Kamenev won the argument for their readmission by arguing:

...the Executive Committee must remember that it was not a party considering its relations with another party, but an organ of government considering the attitude of the country towards a party which in the most serious moment of Russian history had admittedly made grave mistakes and helped Russia's enemies. Now, in this difficult moment, everyone who was sincerely ready to help the working masses of Russia in their struggle had the right to be given a place in the ranks of the fighters. The Social Revolutionaries should be allowed to prove in deeds the sincerity of their recantation.[19]

Notification was made to release imprisoned SRs and allow them to participate in the work of the soviet.

In the same chapter Ransome notes in passing other controversies such as the use of experts in industry, similar to the debate over Trotsky's use of ex-Tsarist officers in the Red Army. He also records the decision to ban the Mensheviks' paper *Vsegda Vpered* '('Forever Forward', but usually described by critics of the Mensheviks as 'Forever Backward') for agitating for an end to the civil war, a demand which was tantamount to calling for capitulation to the Whites. At the same time as the ban, it was made clear it would be lifted as soon as the Mensheviks 'were ready to stand to the defence and support of the revolution'.[20] A failure to do this would simply force the Executive Committee to 'expel them to the territories of Kolchak's democracy.'[21]

So often those who attack the Bolshevik Party omit to tell of the impact on the country of civil war, imperialist intervention and blockades. Those in our time who have watched the same processes at work in Nicaragua, but without the physical invasion experienced by Bolshevik Russia, should surely understand what famine, deprivation and breakdown in the basic economic workings of a country mean for people and democracy. Arthur Ransome certainly did. In fact, *Crisis in Russia* is devoted not only to explaining the real physical state of things and how that affected the workings of democracy he so vividly describes in 1918 and 1919, but to arguing that without the Bolshevik Party the whole country would have collapsed back into barbarism.

Ransome conveys the state of things through small details: 'Soap has become an article so rare that for the present it is to be treated as a means of safeguarding labour to be given to the workmen for washing after and during their work, and in preference to miners, chemical, medical and sanitary workers, for whose efficiency and health it is essential.'[22] Working for the government was so privileged that an acquaintance of Ransome 'who suffered last summer from a slight derangement of the stomach due to improper and inadequate feeding'[23] was prescribed a medicine 'and nearly a dozen different apothecaries were unable to make up the prescription for lack of one or several of the simple ingredients required.'[24]

Ransome also documents the impact of the civil war and the crisis in the economy on the working class and the towns and the way in which workers not caught up in the Red Army or the machinery of government often fled to the countryside simply to survive. The disintegration of the towns further weakened the economy and threatened, as Ransome saw it, 'the first stage of a titanic struggle, with on one side all the forces of nature leading apparently to an inevitable collapse of civilisation, and on the other side nothing but the incalculable force of human will.'[25]

It is perhaps not surprising that, with such a view of conditions in Russia, Ransome sees the Bolshevik Party as the sole mechanism for preventing such a collapse into barbarism. In the chapter 'The Communist Dictatorship' in *Crisis in Russia*, Ransome describes honestly how the Communist Party effectively runs Russia in 1921 and how the lively democracy of the soviets he described in 1918 and 1919 had been replaced by decisions by the central committee of the Communist Party. But he also argues, firstly that what concerned people most who had been cold and hungry for two to three years was inefficiency, secondly that the workings of the Cheka prevented even worse disorder and chaos and finally that the whole lot only functioned because of the lively discussions inside the Communist Party and, as Ransome points out, 'those discussions are the simple fact distinguishing the Communist Dictatorship from any of the other dictatorships by which it may be supplanted.'[26]

Just what Ransome means by that is well illustrated by his next chapter, 'A Conference at Yaroslavl'. Not only does he record the seriousness with which a meeting of workers debated the question of industrial conscription, the principle of one man management in industry and the like, but he remarks on the high level of political awareness in the meeting compared with a few years previously. The meeting also insisted on sending one of its number as a delegate to the forthcoming conference in Moscow despite the fact he had been hopelessly outvoted on the issues up for discussion.

One further chapter in *Crisis in Russia* shows just how right Ransome is to judge the Bolshevik Party quite differently from other dictatorships through his description of the propaganda trains. Of course, it is possible to be perfectly cynical about the sending of trains far and wide across the countryside equipped with cinemas, printing presses and the like, taking the message of the revolution to every corner of that vast country. But it is also possible to see it as part of Bolshevik strategy to persuade, a process which involved raising people's educational level and political understanding and mobilising resources ranging from the country's best artists to the most advanced technology available. Such techniques are not associated with repressive regimes in the midst of civil war.

I have missed out a great deal from Ransome's books, for example his visit to the opera played before hungry workers, and his own observations on seeing a Chekov play in the midst of a revolution. But then hopefully readers of *International Socialism* will avail themselves of the opportunity and go out and buy the new edition.

Just a few parting comments. I suspect the two books will be of most use to people already familiar with the course and debates of the revolution. Apart from the pamphlet 'The Truth about Russia', which provides a history of the revolution, the two books are not written as self contained histories but as contemporary commentaries on events and debates as they were unfolding.[27] As such, I think they are enormously useful, but they assume a working knowledge of the period. There are, inevitably, some irritating omissions such as his views of the Kronstadt rebellion. He was in Russia at the time and believed it had to be repressed, but for some reason decided not to write about it. I also think some of his   sharpest polemics about the civil war and the role of terror in the revolution as well as some of his most vivid portraits of people, situations and other questions are not contained in the books republished by Redwords, but are to be found scattered in his notebooks and papers in the Brotherton Collection in Leeds University. His newspaper articles for the *Daily News* and *The Manchester Guardian* remain to be tapped. Nevertheless, I think we should be more than pleased that these pieces should have been reprinted, even if hopefully some time more of his writings will see the light of day.

Notes

1 'Letter to America', published as 'The Truth about Russia', in A Ransome, *Six Weeks in Russia* (London, 1992) p40.
2 Ibid, p27.
3 Ibid, p51.
4 Ibid, p34.
5 Ibid, p33.
6 Ibid, p41.
7 Ibid, p44.
8 Letter to Gardiner, November 28th, 1918, Ransome Papers, Brotherton Collection, Brotherton Library, Leeds University.
9 Ibid.
10 Ibid.
11 Ibid.
12 *Six Weeks in Russia,* p115.
13 Ibid, p115.
14 Daghestan, Ransome Papers, op cit.
15 Ibid.
16 Ibid.
17 Ibid.
18 Eliava, Ransome Papers, op cit.
19 *Six Weeks*, op cit, p143.
20 Ibid, p144.
21 Ibid, p144.
22 *Crisis in Russia,* (London, 1992), p22.
23 Ibid, p21.
24 Ibid, p22.
25 Ibid, p34.
26 Ibid, p40.
27 'The Truth about Russia' was written consciously as a polemic against allied intervention.

The Socialist Workers Party is one of an international grouping of socialist organisations:

AUSTRALIA: International Socialists, GPO Box 1473N, Melbourne 3001

BELGIUM: Socialisme International, Rue Lovinfosse 60, 4030 Grivengée, Belgium

BRITAIN: Socialist Workers Party, PO Box 82, London E3

CANADA: International Socialists, PO Box 339, Station E, Toronto, Ontario M6H 4E3

DENMARK: Internationale Socialister, Ryesgade 813, 8000 Arhus C, Denmark

FRANCE: Socialisme International, BP 189, 75926 Paris Cedex 19

GERMANY: Sozialistische Arbeitergruppe, Wolfsgangstrasse 81, W-6000 Frankfurt 1

GREECE: Organosi Sosialistiki Epanastasi, c/o Workers Solidarity, PO Box 8161, Athens 100 10, Greece

HOLLAND: International Socialists, PO Box 9720, 3506 GR Utrecht

IRELAND: Socialist Workers Movement, PO Box 1648, Dublin 8

NORWAY: Internasjonale Socialisterr, Postboks 5370, Majorstua, 0304 Oslo 3

POLAND: Solidarność Socjalistyczna, PO Box 12, 01-900 Warszawa 118

SOUTH AFRICA:
International Socialists of South Africa, PO Box 18530, Hillbrow 2038, Johannesburg

UNITED STATES:
International Socialist Organization, PO Box 16085, Chicago, Illinois 60616

The following issues of *International Socialism* (second series) are available price £2.50 (including postage) from IS Journal , PO Box 82, London E3 3LH.

International Socialism 2:54 Spring 1992

Sharon Smith: Twilight of the American dream ★ Mike Haynes: Class and crisis—the transition in eastern Europe ★ Costas Kossis; A miracle without end? Japanese capitalism and the world economy ★ Alex Callinicos: Capitalism and the state system: A reply to Nigel Harris ★ Steven Rose: Do animals have rights? ★ John Charlton: Crime and class in the 18th century ★ John Rees: Revolution, reform and working class culture ★ Chris Harman: Blood simple ★

International Socialism 2:53 Winter 1991

Jonathan Neale: The politics of AIDS ★ Duncan Blackie: Yugoslavia's road to hell ★ Sue Clegg: The remains of Louis Althusser ★ Nigel Harris: A comment on *National Liberation* ★ Alex Callinicos: Drawing the line ★ Conor Kostick: Black struggles and socialism ★ Gareth Jenkins: Honour and anger are not enough ★ Sam Ashman: Gramsci's political thought revisited ★

International Socialism 2:52 Autumn 1991

John Rees: In defence of October ★ Ian Taylor and Julie Waterson: The political crisis in Greece, an interview with Maria Styllou and Panos Garganas ★ Paul McGarr: Mozart, overture to revolution ★ Lee Humber: Class, class consciousness and the English Revolution ★ Derek Howl: The legacy of Hal Draper ★

International Socialism 2:51 Summer 1991

Chris Harman: The state and capitalism today ★ Alex Callinicos: The end of nationalism? ★ Sharon Smith: Feminists for a strong state? ★ Colin Sparks and Sue Cockerill: Goodbye to the Swedish miracle ★ Simon Phillips: The South African Communist Party and the South African working class ★ John Brown: Class conflict and the crisis of feudalism ★

International Socialism 2:49 Winter 1990

Chris Bambery: The decline of the Western Communist Parties ★ Ernest Mandel: A theory which has not withstood the test of time ★ Chris Harman: Criticism which does not withstand the test of logic ★ Derek Howl: The law of value In the USSR ★ Terry Eagleton: Shakespeare and the class struggle ★ Lionel Sims: Rape and pre-state societies ★ Sheila McGregor A reply to Lionel Sims ★

International Socialism 2:48 Autumn 1990

Lindsey German: The last days of Thatcher ★ John Rees: The new imperialism ★ Neil Davidson and Donny Gluckstein: Nationalism and the class struggle In Scotland ★ Paul McGarr: Order out of chaos ★

International Socialism 2:47 Summer 1990

Ahmed Shawki: Black liberation and socialism in the United States ★ Fifty years since Trotsky's death ★ John Rees: Trotsky and the dialectic ★ Chris Harman: From Trotsky to state capitalism ★ Steve Wright: Hal Draper's' Marxism ★

International Socialism 2:46 Winter 1989

Chris Harman: The storm breaks ★ Alex Callinicos: Can South Africa be reformed? ★ John Saville: Britain, the Marshall Plan and the Cold War ★ Sue Clegg: Against the stream ★ John Rees: The rising bourgeoisie ★

International Socialism 2:45 Autumn 1989

Sheila McGregor: Rape, pornography and capitalism ★ Boris Kagarlitsky: The market instead of democracy? ★ Chris Harman: From feudalism to capitalism ★ plus Mike Gonzalez and Sabby Sagall discuss Central America ★

International Socialism 2:44 Autumn 1989

Charlie Hore: China: Tiananmen Square and after ★ Sue Clegg: Thatcher and the welfare state ★ John Molyneux: *Animal Farm* revisited ★ David Finkel: After Arias, is the revolution over? ★ John Rose: Jews in Poland ★

International Socialism 2:42 Spring 1989

Chris Harman: The myth of market socialism ★ Norah Carlin: Roots of gay oppression ★ Duncan Blackie: Revolution in science ★ International Socialism Index ★

International Socialism 2:41 Winter 1988
Polish socialists speak out: Solidarity at the Crossroads ★ Mike Haynes: Nightmares of the market ★ Jack Robertson: Socialists and the unions ★ Andy Strouthous: Are the unions in decline? ★ Richard Bradbury What is Post-Structuralism? ★ Colin Sparks: George Bernard Shaw ★

International Socialism 2:40 Autumn 1988
Phil Marshall: Islamic fundamentalism—oppression and revolution ★ Duncan Hallas: Trotsky's heritage—on the 50th anniversary of the founding of the Fourth International ★ Ann Rogers: Is there a new underclass? ★ Colin Sparks: The origins of Shakespeare's drama ★ Mike Gonzalez: Introduction to John Berger on Picasso ★ John Berger Defending Picasso's late work ★ Alex Callinicos: The foundations of Athenian democracy ★ Norah Carlin: Reply to Callinicos ★

International Socialism 2:39 Summer 1988
Chris Harman and Andy Zebrowski: Glasnost, before the storm ★ Chanie Rosenberg: Labour and the fight against fascism ★ Mike Gonzalez: Central America after the Peace Plan ★ Ian Birchall: Raymond Williams ★ Alex Callinicos: Reply to John Rees ★

International Socialism 2:36 Autumn 1987
Dave Beecham and Ann Eidenham: Beyond the mass strike—class, state and party in Brazil ★ Chris Bambery :The politics of James P Cannon ★ Norah Carlin: Was there racism in ancient society? ★ Paul Kellogg: Goodbye to the working class ★ Lutte Ouvrière: A critique of the SWP Analysis of the French railway workers' strike ★ Gareth Jenkins: A reply to Lutte Ouvrière ★ Ian Birchall: A comment on Colin Sparks on film theory ★

International Socialism 2:35 Summer 1987
Pete Green: Capitalism and the Thatcher years ★ Alex Callinicos: Imperialism, capitalism and the state today ★ Ian Birchall: Five years of *New Socialist* ★ Callinicos and Wood debate 'Looking for alternatives to reformism' ★ David Widgery replies on 'Beating Time' ★

International Socialism 2:31 Winter 1985
Alex Callinicos: Marxism and revolution In South Africa ★ Tony Cliff: The tragedy of A J Cook ★ Nigel Harris: What to do with London? The strategies of the GLC ★

International Socialism 2:30 Autumn 1985
Gareth Jenkins: Where is the Labour Party heading? ★ David McNally: Debt, inflation and the rate of profit ★ Ian Birchall: The terminal crisis in the British Communist Party ★ replies on Women's oppression and *Marxism Today* ★

International Socialism 2:29 Summer 1985
Special issue on the class struggle and the left in the aftermath of the miners' defeat ★ Tony Cliff: Patterns of mass strike ★ Chris Harman: 1984 and the shape of things to come ★ Alex Callinicos: The politics of *Marxism Today* ★

International Socialism 2:27 & 28
Special double issue published in conjunction with Socialist Worker ★ Alex Callinicos and Mike Simons on ★ The Great Strike: the Miners' Strike of 1984-5 and its lessons ★

International Socialism 2:26 Spring 1985
Pete Green: Contradictions of the American boom ★ Colin Sparks: Labour and imperialism ★ Chris Bambery: Marx and Engels and the unions ★ Sue Cockerill: The municipal road to socialism ★ Norah Carlin: Is the family part of the superstructure? ★ Kieran Allen: James Connolly and the 1916 rebellion ★

International Socialism 2:25 Autumn 1984
John Newsinger: Jim Larkin, Syndicalism and the 1913 Dublin Lockout ★ Pete Binns: Revolution and state capitalism in the Third World ★ Colin Sparks: Towards a police state? ★ Dave Lyddon: Demystifying the downturn ★ John Molyneux: Do working class men benefit from women's oppression? ★

International Socialism 2:18 Winter 1983
Donny Gluckstein: Workers' councils in Western Europe ★ Jane Ure Smith: The early Communist press in Britain ★ John Newsinger: The Bolivian Revolution ★ Andy Durgan: Largo Caballero and Spanish socialism ★ M Barker and A Beezer: Scarman and the language of racism ★

International Socialism 2:14 Winter 1981
Chris Harman: The riots of 1981 ★ Dave Beecham: Class struggle under the Tories ★ Tony Cliff: Alexandra Kollontai ★ L James and A Paczuska: Socialism needs feminism ★ reply to Cliff on Zetkin ★ Feminists In the labour movement ★